P9-DNB-798

A NOTE TO THE READER

This publication has been electronically reproduced from digital information. Jossey-Bass is pleased to make use of this technology to keep works of enduring value in print as long as there is a reasonable demand to do so. The content of this book is identical to previous printings.

Leadership for the Emerging Age

Jerold W. Apps

Leadership for the Emerging Age

Transforming Practice in Adult and Continuing Education

Jossey-Bass Publishers
San Francisco

Copyright © 1994 by Jossey-Bass Inc., Publishers, 350 Sansome Street,
San Francisco, California 94104.
All rights reserved. No part of this publication may be reproduced, stored in
a retrieval system, or transmitted, in any form or by any means, electronic,
mechanical, photocopying, recording, or otherwise, without the prior
written permission of the publisher.

Substantial discounts on bulk quantities of Jossey-Bass books
are available to corporations, professional associations, and
other organizations. For details and discount information,
contact the special sales department at Jossey-Bass Inc.,
Publishers. (415) 433–1740; Fax (415) 433–0499.

Manufactured in the United States of America

Jossey-Bass Web address: http://www.josseybass.com

Library of Congress Cataloging-in-Publication Data

Apps, Jerold W., date.
   Leadership for the emerging age: transforming practice in adult and
continuing education/Jerold W. Apps. — 1st ed.
     p.   cm. — (The Jossey-Bass higher and adult education series)
   Includes bibliographical references and index.
   ISBN–0–7879–0036–2
   1. Educational leadership—United States. 2. Adult education—
United States—Administration. I. Title. II. Series.
LC5225.A34A67   1994
374'.12—dc20   94–27619
                                                         CIP

First Edition
HB Printing 10 9 8 7 6 5 4 3   *Code 94118*

The Jossey-Bass

Higher and Adult Education Series

Consulting Editor
Adult and Continuing Education

Alan B. Knox
University of Wisconsin, Madison

Contents

x   Contents

Preface

We are now living in the most challenging and perplexing times that leaders in adult education have ever faced. Adult and continuing education organizations are asked to program in new ways, to reach new and often overlooked audiences, to provide learning opportunities that include distance learning technologies as well as traditional approaches, and to provide offerings that meet a new and higher standard of quality.

Adult education leaders face challenges, frustrations, ambiguity, and even chaos. Many of these challenges arise from the emergence of a new social era that is replacing the industrial age, which has influenced all of society's institutions for generations. This emerging age demands that adult and continuing education organizations—and other groups, too—change dramatically. Many adult and continuing education organizations are riding this wave—structuring themselves differently and programming in innovative ways.

The changes will likely occur over a lengthy period, fostering long-term uncertainty and apprehension. A new kind of leader, with a new approach to leadership, is essential for adult and continuing education organizations to work through these changes.

The purpose of this book is threefold: (1) to examine the characteristics of this new era we are experiencing and its implications for adult education; (2) to explore the dimensions of a leadership approach that fits the times; and (3) to provide a series of practical suggestions for people who want to become leaders in the emerging age.

The book is written for leaders who work in an array of adult and continuing education organizations, including the Cooperative Extension Service, youth organizations, technical colleges, libraries, college and university extension divisions, museums, community organizations, for-profit adult education organizations, and literacy and job-training programs. The term *leader* is defined broadly. This book is for organizational leaders at every level, from program leaders to directors, deans, departmental chairs, provosts, and executive heads. In the emerging age, everyone in an organization is a leader, although some will have greater administrative responsibilities than others. This book is also for graduate students studying adult education administration and leadership and for participants in leadership development workshops.

At another level, this book is for leaders who are now in administrative leadership positions but are searching for a new way of leading, given the pressures and challenges of the times. It is also for adult educators who aspire to administrative leadership roles and want some direction about how to proceed. Students studying leadership in formal graduate and undergraduate courses will find this book useful as a guide to understanding the new requirements for leadership in adult and continuing education, as well as approaches for developing as leaders.

Overview of Contents

In Chapter One I point out that adult and continuing education organizations are culture bound, relying on traditions with roots in the military, the church, and the corporation. I then introduce some of the unique perspectives for a new approach to leadership that has its foundation in the arts, humanities, and sciences.

Chapter Two includes an examination of a new perspective that has become part of society. This new perspective, referred to as the emerging age, requires leaders in adult and continuing education to think in new ways, frame problems differently, and explore new assumptions.

In Chapter Three I consider historical and contemporary perspectives on leadership, discuss leadership myths that must be dispelled, and describe a new kind of leadership for adult and continuing education.

Chapter Four outlines a process for writing a personal philosophy of leadership. The process includes a study of organizational contexts, mind-body-spirit relationships, and fundamental beliefs about reality, people, knowledge, ethics, and aesthetics; and it emphasizes leader qualities and characteristics, leadership approaches, outcomes for leadership, and educational perspectives. This chapter also includes discussion of and approaches for writing a personal credo statement.

Leadership beliefs and values are the topic of Chapter Five. Beliefs and values are the essence of a personal leadership philosophy. In this chapter I describe a process for examining personal beliefs and values and point out that they may sometimes be contradicted by our actions.

Chapter Six begins with an examination of several metaphors for adult education leaders. It proceeds to explore the qualities and characteristics that will be required of leaders in this time of transition.

In Chapter Seven I discuss leadership outcomes, especially those expected in the emerging age. Vision and mission statements are also reviewed in this chapter.

Chapter Eight is about approaches to leadership, with particular attention given to gender differences and the uses of power in leadership.

In Chapter Nine I focus on educational perspectives and the ways in which they are changing during the emerging age. I discuss adult teaching, teachers, learning, and learners.

Taking charge of your own development is the subject of Chapter Ten, with attention given especially to developing a personal learning plan, keeping a journal, and taking time for reflection.

Chapter Eleven is about the process of transformation, what it is and how it applies to leadership development.

Finally, in Chapter Twelve I discuss some of the challenges for adult and continuing education leaders and organizations. I also offer several suggestions for organizing and operating leadership development programs.

Acknowledgments

Many people helped me with this book, in a variety of ways. In the early planning stages, Henry Spille, vice president and director of the Center for Adult Learning and Educational Credentials, American Council on Education; Barbara Warren, of the University of Minnesota Extension; Donald Campbell, director of Continuing Education and Extension at the University of Wisconsin, La Crosse; and William Draves, executive director of the Learning Resources Network, offered valuable criticism and raised many questions.

Participants in the leadership workshops I have conducted throughout the United States, Canada, Mexico, and Europe made many suggestions for sharpening the ideas and approaches that were used in the workshops and that are now presented in this book. I especially want to recognize the seventy interns (Classes I, II, and III) who participated in the National Extension Leadership Development (NELD) program, which I directed for several years, sponsored in part by the W. K. Kellogg Foundation. These interns took part in workshops held in classrooms and canoes, on Indian reservations, in a Mexico City conference center, and in African/American homes in central Alabama, among other places. I especially want to thank them for encouraging me to continue helping leaders develop personal philosophies and credo statements and to recognize the importance of mind-body-spirit relationships.

The NELD staff—Boyd Rossing, Tim Neuman, and especially Judy Adrian, all with the University of Wisconsin—helped me more than they will ever know to express thoughts that I felt strongly about but sometimes had difficulty communicating.

Others who helped, particularly in the later stages of the book's development, include Alan Knox, consulting editor, who imparted many useful suggestions for revising the manuscript, and my wife, Ruth, who offered helpful comments on several chapters.

Madison, Wisconsin   Jerold W. Apps
May 1994

The Author

Jerold W. Apps is a writer and an educational consultant for adult and continuing education. Until recently he was professor of adult and continuing education and chairperson of the Department of Continuing and Vocational Education at the University of Wisconsin, Madison. He received his B.S. degree (1955) and his M.S. degree (1957) in agricultural education and his Ph.D. (1967) in adult education from the University of Wisconsin.

Apps's research focuses on leadership in adult education, future directions, and new approaches to adult learning. In 1982 he won the Research to Practice Award presented by the Adult Education Association of the United States for his research and writings in adult and continuing education. In 1987 he received the Outstanding Leadership Award presented by the Wisconsin Association for Adult and Continuing Education for his research and writings. In 1988 Apps was Distinguished Visiting Professor at the University of Alberta, and in 1990 he was Lansdowne Scholar at the University of Victoria. His books include *Redefining the Discipline of Adult Education* (1980, with Robert D. Boyd), *The Adult Learner on Campus* (1981), *Improving Practice in Continuing Education: Modern Approaches for Understanding the Field and Determining Priorities* (1985), *Higher Education in a Learning Society* (1988), and *Mastering the Teaching of Adults* (1991).

Chapter One

Uprooting a Leadership Tradition

Leadership is not what it used to be—and likely never was. As absurd as that statement may sound, in many ways it describes the situation that leaders in adult education organizations face these days. Uncertainty, ambiguity, frustration, and even chaos are reality for many leaders in adult education organizations. We have reached a time when most traditional approaches to leading simply do not work anymore. The call is for new approaches and new thinking about leaders and leading and about adult education organizations and their visions and structures.

Paul Edelson (1992) points out how culture bound leadership in adult and continuing education can be. Adult and continuing education, he writes, are "heavily influenced by the traditions passed on . . . [by] the military, the church, and the corporation. The first two in particular, because of their historical persistence over thousands of years, have become organizational archetypes and serve as models for how we frame our thinking about organizations today" (p. 6). Throughout this book I argue for new approaches to leading. I also offer several approaches for becoming the new kind of leader that the emerging age of adult education demands.

When I was eighteen years old, I applied for a summer job at a cucumber-salting station. At a salting station, workers receive cucumbers from growers, sort and grade them, and then dump them into huge vats with carefully measured amounts of water and salt. After I had been hired, the regional manager asked if I'd like to manage the station. He informed me that I'd receive twenty-five

1

ticipants were bringing to me. I also began to see glimmers of new approaches to leadership. Many of these new ideas were coming out of the private sector, where tough economic times, including global competition and changing consumer demands, were forcing many firms to look at new approaches for everything they did. These new approaches also demanded new strategies for leadership.

When I became chair of my university department I discovered many similarities with the cucumber-salting station, and many differences as well (during my tour there were no faculty fistfights). The challenge in both situations was to make sure that the work was done and was of high quality, and to contend with calamities that regularly appeared. Two days of rain and the salting station stopped. I sent the men home until the migrant workers could once more return to the cucumber fields. Then we worked around the clock for several days as we tried to catch up with the rapidly maturing crop. Soon we were all in a survival mode, trying to maintain enough physical energy to keep going as the spiny cucumbers, like a never-ending river of green, continued bouncing along the conveyor belt. After the first year, I often thought about improving how we did things, and I had a chance to introduce a few new ideas. But too many crises occurred for me to do much thinking about new approaches.

As a university department chair I faced a host of challenges, including severe budget cuts and threats of more, a decrease in secretarial support, and demands from the community for more practical courses for community adult educators. Increasingly I worked from one crisis to the next. I felt like an appliance "fix-it" person. No sooner did I help fix one problem than another came along. When was I supposed to be a leader, I wondered? And what did it mean to be a leader during rapidly changing times with unending trials and unforeseen problems? During those years I tried to look at bigger pictures and longer-range perspectives, approaches that I knew were important and necessary. But I hadn't figured out how to handle the crisis of the moment so that I'd have time to focus on future directions, develop relationships with other units, make contacts with community organizations, and the like.

More recently, I headed a W. K. Kellogg Foundation–supported leadership development program called National Extension Leadership Development (NELD). A small staff and I offered a two-year leadership development program for middle managers in continuing education and extension programs and for a number of persons outside of universities who were recruited as a part of each leadership class. We held four weeklong (and sometimes longer) workshops for each class. Participants also developed special projects at their home institutions, read extensively, and planned a variety of activities for themselves. In addition to the middle manager group, we conducted workshops for deans and directors of extension and continuing education programs from across the country.

Early in this leadership development program, I discovered several things. In the minds of many of the participants, leadership positions had come under even greater pressure than I remembered from my last administrative assignment. Several of the participants told of the long hours they worked and of the harmful effects their work was having on their spouses and families. Some lamented that simply working harder was not making much difference either. The harder they worked and the more hours they put in, the more work accumulated, it seemed. I could see the toll that stress and pressure were taking on these individuals. Some participants, arriving at a weeklong workshop on Sunday, didn't even begin to relax until Tuesday. During breaks they rushed to the phones and fax machines, and during sessions they scribbled notes to themselves; some even tried writing memos and letters.

Many of these adult and continuing education leaders were familiar with the current books on leadership theory and practice. Some even carried these books with them for "airplane reading." But something was missing. What was missing, I concluded, was a "whole person" approach to leadership, an approach that combined thinking and feeling, matters of the head and matters of the heart.

At the core of this approach is for leaders to have a well-thought-out personal philosophy of leadership. I have seen the value of a personal philosophy in other settings. For many years I taught graduate classes to help adult education leaders develop personal philosophies. I often hear from these graduate students how much the process of developing a personal philosophy helped them straighten out what they valued and believed, and in turn helped them make better sense of their work.

After contacts with several hundred adult and continuing education leaders over the course of several years, it became clear to me that a new approach to leadership and leadership development was necessary. Some of the leadership literature had pointed the way: Burns (1978) and Bass (1990) shared ideas about transformational leadership; Vaill (1989) and De Pree (1989) argued that leadership is an art as well as a science; and more recently, Covey (1991), Drucker (1992), Gardner (1990), Kouzes and Posner (1990), Nanus (1992), Senge (1990), Wheatley (1992), and others have suggested several new ways for thinking about leadership.

As I explain in Chapter Two in some depth, times are changing, and the requirements for leadership are changing as well. What I call the emerging age is here and will likely be with us for an extended time. It is a time of confusion and frustration, of disappointment and challenge. It is a time of lightning-fast change of a kind that many of us have not experienced before. It is a time when new adult education organizations and arrangements are emerging, old ones are disappearing, and all are constantly redirecting and restructuring. It is a time when old rules for leading do not work well, if at all, but the new rules are not yet written.

Today's current and aspiring adult education leaders will write these new rules for leading. They will discover the leadership required for the emerging age, sometimes through sheer boldness and risk taking, other times through patience and perseverance.

It has become clear to me that a "technical" approach to leading based on lists of skills to develop and recipes to follow will no longer suffice, if it ever did. Leadership development for the emerging age is ongoing and lifelong, like all learning and development. The struggle to develop as a leader is never-ending.

The unique perspective this book offers for leading and leadership development is its emphasis on the value of a personal philosophy of leadership, and approaches for developing one. A personal philosophy of leadership provides the core for leaders facing new times and challenges. A personal philosophy shows people how to be whole, how to draw on the deepest dimensions of who they are, and how to lead lives that include families and outside interests, as well as a commitment to work and organization.

I have built on the research and scholarship about leadership as well as on my own research and experience. I regard this book as a blueprint for developing a new approach to leadership and a new way of defining leaders in adult and continuing education.

Perspectives on a New Approach to Leadership

The approach to leadership in this book takes the following perspectives:

• *We are clearly in a new time,* a time I call the emerging age, in which old solutions to problems and old leadership strategies often do not work. The emerging age of adult education requires fundamentally new ways of thinking about adult learning and teaching, about the relationship between individual and "organizational" learning, and about such fundamental concerns as efficiency and effectiveness, the nature of knowledge, and linear and nonlinear approaches to action.

• *In this emerging age, adult education organizations and their leaders need stability but are also challenged to change.* Stability, for many leaders, resides in having a well-thought-out personal philosophy of leadership. Knowing one's fundamental beliefs and values, and understanding leader qualities and characteristics, leadership outcomes, leadership approaches, and educational perspectives comprise the components of a personal philosophy of leadership. A leadership philosophy can provide bedrock security during times of chaotic change and upheaval.

• *Management and leadership are related but are not the same.* Too often in the past, adult educators talked about management functions such as budgeting, program planning, and evaluation as if they were leadership functions. They are not. Too often leadership— what it is and how it is performed—has been lost in the flurry of management articles and books.

• *Much of leadership in the emerging age is paradoxical.* Opposing ideas come together in what appear to be absurd relationships; for instance, we often do more by doing less, and we gain power by giving it away.

• *Leadership is based on a local context as well as on a broader societal context that includes a global perspective.* These two contexts often conflict. Yet the leader is responsible for responding to both contexts. The broader context represents the challenges of the emerging age. The local context often represents what has existed for some time.

• *Leaders for the emerging age must develop a capacity for leadership that goes beyond gaining leadership skills.* Leadership capacity is the ability to lead in unknown, difficult situations where reliable information and well-thought-out strategies are not available. Leadership capacity combines certain skills with calm and assuredness when chaos seems to prevail. It also encompasses a bent toward inventing and trying new approaches when unique situations are encountered.

• *Leaders for the emerging age must become continual, reflective, self-directed learners and practitioners who are able to examine the con-*

text in which they work and make adjustments in what they do on the basis of this examination. In rapidly changing conditions, leaders constantly invent and reinvent leadership approaches.

• *Leaders must find their own voice.* Leading is a very personal activity, even though it is done in concert with others. A leader can learn from other leaders but ultimately must develop a uniquely suitable personal leadership approach.

• *Story and metaphor, as approaches to understanding and communicating ideas about leadership, allow for nuances of meaning that go beyond linear or technical approaches to leadership.*

• *Leadership for the emerging age has its roots in a joining of the arts, humanities, and sciences.* It accepts the findings of scientific researchers who have studied leadership. It also embraces the work of artists and philosophers who see the world in a different way.

• *Learning leadership is an ongoing process, never static, always in flux.* Leaders must take charge of their own development, relying on such aids as learning plans, journaling, developing personal history statements, seeking solitude, and learning how to reflect on their personal experiences.

• *Becoming a leader for the emerging age of adult education involves a transformation for most people, for the organizations where they work, and for the people the organizations serve.* Transformation is highly personal, often touching the core of what people believe and value and requiring a transition that can be both trying and satisfying.

• *As individuals attempt to become different kinds of leaders, not only are they personally challenged, but the persons with whom they come into contact, both inside and outside the organization, are challenged as well.*

The foundation for the approach to leadership suggested here builds on the leadership research and scholarship of the past but also sets out in new and occasionally radical directions. Leaders for the emerging age of adult education will have to invent many of the leadership approaches they use as they are using them. The key to their success will be building leadership capacity. Basic to leadership capacity is a well-understood and well-developed philosophy of leadership, including knowledge of one's personal beliefs and values.

Chapter Two

Changing with the Emerging Age

The perspective that has guided adult education for the past fifty years or so is changing. This long-lived perspective has allowed adult education leaders to get up in the morning and know what to do: how to plan programs, how to attract participants, how to teach effectively, how to supervise employees, how to please stakeholders, and a host of other tasks. The old perspective on adult education shaped what we believed about people, about knowledge, and about change and how it occurs. It gave adult education leaders a framework for thinking and a blueprint for action. But the old perspective is not working so well anymore.

Recently I talked with an administrator of university extension–sponsored writing programs. She had organized a noncredit course on life story writing that met for two hours every Tuesday evening for five weeks. It was a tried-and-true model, used hundreds of times with considerable success. But the format no longer worked well. The instructors were competent, the subject matter was compelling, and participants were interested, yet only a half dozen participants enrolled in a recent class. The administrator gave the program the go-ahead, hoping that this was merely one more exception to the long-standing approach to programming. But it wasn't. By the end of the five-week sessions, only three students continued to participate. They said they would prefer some other approach, maybe something that could be done electronically so they wouldn't have to leave home.

A New Perspective Emerging

A new perspective is emerging in adult education. Put more accurately, we are between perspectives. We are leaving a perspective that we knew and had become comfortable with and moving toward a new perspective that is appearing on the horizon.

Of course, not only adult education is facing a new perspective. All of society is leaving behind a time that defined our reality and provided us with an understanding of how the world works. By way of background, over the centuries of history, human beings have divided time into eras or ages. We are quite familiar with the stone age, the dark ages, the age of the hunter, the middle ages, the agrarian age, and the industrial age. Key events moved us from one age to another; for example, the invention of first the steam engine and then the internal combustion engine and the harnessing of electricity helped move us from the agrarian age to the industrial age. Such movements from age to age had far more influence on people than just the easily observable changes—the development of new modes of transportation and communication that were part of the movement into the industrial age, for example. Not only did automobiles appear in the industrial age, but the way in which we thought about distance, trails (roads), and time changed. Many of our society's institutions and structures strained under the changes. Small community businesses within a couple of hours of travel by horse-drawn buggy closed down as it became possible for people to travel many more miles in two hours in a "horseless carriage."

When we move from age to age, the most fundamental characteristics of what we believe and value often change. For example, Fritjof Capra (1983) says the assumptions of the old perspective, the age we are leaving behind, include "the belief in the scientific method as the only valid approach to knowledge; the view of the universe as a mechanical system composed of elementary building blocks; the view of life in society as a competitive struggle for existence; and the belief in unlimited progress to be achieved through economic and technological growth" (p. 31).

A more specific example is how the view of time has changed from age to age. The concept of time had a different meaning in the industrial age compared to the agrarian age. In the agrarian age, when the majority of the people lived on the land, time meant sunrise and sunset, the full moon and the new moon, fall changing to winter. In the industrial age, time became a commodity that was bought and sold. We began measuring time in hours and recording them and paying people for the hours they spent working rather than for the task that was to be accomplished.

As we move from age to age, some elements of the previous age continue. We don't cut all ties with the previous age in favor of the new. In some adult education settings, the programming approach outlined above for the writing course will continue to be successful. Some people will continue wanting a face-to-face experience and a more leisurely approach to writing that allows them a week to work on assignments. But in many situations this programming approach will beg for an alternative that is more in accord with the emerging perspective on adult education.

In a more global perspective, we can find elements of earlier ages. The Amish people in Lancaster, Pennsylvania, and many other places in this country have successfully avoided most aspects of the industrial age. They farm with horses, have no electricity, and avoid contact with "modern conveniences." Other countries of the world have large agrarian societies but may encourage industrial production as well.

In the more developed countries of the world, we see the movement from the industrial age to something else, a new age not clearly focused. Writers have difficulty defining the time into which we are moving. Walter Anderson (1990) says we are moving into a world that no longer knows how to define itself, except in terms of what it is not. We hear about a postindustrial society and a postmodern age. Others refer to this emerging era as the information age, the knowledge age, the communication age, or the global age.

I call this new perspective that we are moving into the "emerging age," meaning that we are clearly moving beyond the world that the industrial revolution wrought. It is not necessary, at least for me, to label this new era specifically, other than to acknowledge that it is a time different from the past, a new perspective. Such labeling may in any case be premature and ultimately confining. I would prefer to see the emerging age unfold on its own rather than try to force it into some defined and labeled box the dimensions of which we do not yet know. The emerging age is not entirely a new age, as some would like to name it. Almost paradoxically, it has elements of the present and the past but is also profoundly different.

Characteristics of the Emerging Age

It is possible to look at the emerging age at several levels. The following are easily observable examples of characteristics that influence not only society in general but adult education activity as well.

• *Political changes are occurring nearly everywhere.* Eastern European countries wrestle with internal strife and conflict, often resulting in bloody confrontations. More people are realizing that they belong to both a local community (an ethnic group, a religious group, a geographic area, a specific village or state) and a global community. Local and global interests often conflict as the world's people struggle to become a global community while maintaining their unique and special local cultures. Increasingly, adult education programs are focusing on global concerns, recognizing that everyone is simultaneously a citizen of the world and a member of a local society.

• *A world economic community is emerging.* Unfortunately, many people view the concept of global community solely as an economic issue, failing to realize that religious, historical, social, and political perspectives come into play in a global economic community. World economic issues focus on global economic competition and comparative advantage—how can the countries of the world compete more effectively in a global economic environment? Unfortunately, such discussions seldom embrace concern for the weaker, less fortunate countries that have little or no competitive clout with the world's economic giants.

The countries of the European Union are committed to a new and more unified approach to world marketing, but certainly not without struggle. North America's three nations—Canada, the United States, and Mexico—are attempting to forge new alliances for free trade and as a result stimulate new ideas about economics and the world, and sensitize us to environmental abuse, inequality of workers, and a host of other questions.

- *Nagging world problems continue*—hunger in many places in the world, environmental threats and destruction that have taken on global importance, illiteracy (a growing concern in the United States), violations of human rights, problems of U.S. inner cities, people without homes or jobs, substance abuse, crime, the collapse of the family, and a host of others.

- *Technology is increasing ever more rapidly.* Computer chips are secreted in everything from watches to automobiles. Biotechnology creates frost-resistant crops and medical drugs. Technology is rapidly transforming how information is stored, transmitted, and retrieved. Information travels freely around the world. Recently, when I was traveling with a leadership group in Europe, members of our group and our hosts watched the daily news on CNN and discussed what was happening in the world.

Thousands of people have computer on-line services that let them talk via computer. Entire libraries of information are now available on international computer databases. Even though many people have access to these resources and readily use them, the downside is that there are millions of people who do not have access to these vast information resources, because of illiteracy, low income, political subjugation, and a host of other reasons. The information revolution has encouraged a larger-than-ever chasm between the information haves and the information have-nots.

Another less than bright side to the information revolution concerns people who mistakenly equate collecting information with learning. Learning is deeper and broader than merely collecting information that is somehow applied to problem solving, skill building, or other challenges that individuals and society face. Because of the information revolution (and for other reasons, too), teaching is taking on new dimensions, as is the role of the teacher.

• *The population of this country and several other developed countries is becoming increasingly older.* According to the U.S. Bureau of the Census (1989), Americans aged sixty-five and older will increase by 30 percent between 2010 and 2020. In the year 2000, almost one-third of the population will be fifty or older. Vast differences in educational needs will exist. Millions of adults will continue to seek learning to enhance job skills and economic opportunities. But millions of others will seek education for non-job-related reasons—searching for a deeper meaning in life, learning in order to improve communities and protect the environment, or learning for the sheer joy of it.

Robert Hutchins (1968), former president of the University of Chicago, described what we are seeing now as a learning society. He said that a learning society is "one that, in addition to offering part-time adult education to every man and woman at every stage of grown-up life, had succeeded in transforming its values in such a way that learning, fulfillment, becoming human had become its aims, and all its institutions were directed toward that end" (pp. 164–165).

Many adults these days are seeking not just part-time educational opportunities but also full-time opportunities, with gaining

degrees as a goal. Learning for people of every age has become ubiq-
uitous; like breathing, it is integral to life. We learn as we earn, but
we also learn as we live. As Eduard Lindeman ([1926] 1961, pp.
4–5) reminded us many years ago, learning *is* life, not a preparation
for some future existence.

• *Taxpayers are increasingly questioning the goals and activities of
tax-supported adult education organizations, as well as all other tax-
supported educational activities.* The challenge is to make programs
more relevant and keep costs down. For-profit educational activity, too, feels ever-increasing pressure to provide relevant programs
of high quality or face extinction. For example, an East
Coast–based adult education organization offered workshops on
everything from belly dancing to approaches for intelligent investing. A consumer-conscious public soon discovered that many of its
courses lacked quality, and the organization folded.

• *New adult education organizations are emerging in many communities.* Some are tax-supported; many are not. Some are nonprofit; others are profit oriented. The result is that adults in these
communities have a clear choice as to where they go for learning
opportunities. In my home community of Madison, Wisconsin, it
is possible to study everything from Tai Chi to weight loss, from
business writing to controlling stress, and from money management
to developing self-esteem through outdoor challenge courses. All
of these are offered by adult education organizations not affiliated
with any university, college, or technical school.

• *Adult education participants, actual and potential, are placing
increasing pressure on providers for quality.* As Leonard Freedman
(1987) observes, we are at a point where quality itself must be rede-
fined. He argues that many providers have too long defined quality on the basis of the front end of the equation (teachers'
credentials, numbers of books in the library, institutional reputa-
tion, accreditation, and the like) rather than on the benefits to

learners from participation. Newer definitions of quality focus on such questions as how the experience has assisted the learner—to gain a new perspective, to find new meaning, to develop some skill, to prepare for a particular job, and so on (Apps, 1991).

New Thinking Needed

Not only does adult education face changing conditions, but more fundamental changes are in the wind as well. Adult education leadership for the emerging age requires more than a knowledge of changing conditions in society. It requires attention to a new set of assumptions that are emerging. The new perspective on adult education has a different foundation than the old one with which many of us have become comfortable. This new perspective on adult education leadership is shifting from a mechanistic attitude marked by objectivity, control, predictability, competition, efficiency, and single views of knowledge to an attitude that values context, shared power, multiple relationships, and varied knowledge sources in which predictability is often impossible.

The new perspective on adult education leadership requires a new metaphor. The old metaphor was one of a machine, of components that operate in a linear fashion and outcomes that are predictable. The new metaphor is one of a living organism—extremely complex, unpredictable, and interconnected with other organisms.

To move to a new set of assumptions and to embrace the new perspective on adult education leadership require a new way of thinking. But most of us resist tampering with something as basic as how we think. The tendency is to continue doing as we have done in the past. We believe, most often erroneously, that with a little fine-tuning our current thinking about leadership will continue to serve us well. Some of it will; much of it will not.

Ian Mitroff (1988) writes, "On every front of our existence, the problems the United States faces today cannot even be properly defined, let alone solved in terms of the old prevailing solutions. In short, the old solutions just don't work anymore" (p. 3). He goes on to say that the old solutions are the products of outdated ways of thinking.

Not only do the old solutions not fit the problems and challenges of the day, but they do not allow us to view the changes that occur around us in new and innovative ways. The emerging age, as a result, requires new ways of thinking and doing. For example, I recently learned of a state cooperative extension organization that was rethinking its use of district directors, middle managers who supervised field staff in various regions of the state. One of the current district directors retired, and the state director immediately suggested appointing a committee to find a replacement for the position. This director believed that district directors were important to the success of his organization, and an alternative to this arrangement did not occur to him. Further, he believed, without ever thinking about an alternative, that he was in charge, the associate director was next in charge, and then came the district directors—all neat and tidy. Everyone knew whom to report to, and everyone knew what was expected.

Several field staffers visited the district director and asked if he would listen to an alternative. The state director was curious because in his mind there was no alternative, and the sooner the position was filled, the better.

The staff members suggested that the position not be filled and that the money saved be used to support educational programs in the district. After several budget cuts, many important programs were suffering. The staffers said, "Let us appoint a team of staff members from our district to do what the district director did."

After considerable discussion over a period of weeks, the state director said he would try the approach for a year, to see how it worked. At this writing, the experiment is midway through its first year, and it seems to be successful. On the plus side, there is great excitement and high staff morale in the district. The staff feel that they now have much more say about how they program and with whom. The very essence of the approach challenges an old assumption about power and who has it. In this instance, the state director did not appoint the district director; the field staff took on the leadership responsibility for appointing a team to serve instead.

As adult education agencies, organizations, and institutions and their leaders look ahead with the hope of becoming more responsive to individual and societal problems, examination of their basic assumptions and their approaches to thinking can assist them in discovering a new way.

Approach to Thinking

The old perspective on adult education leadership and adult education programming was one of dichotomies, of either-or, of for and against. Some people argued for the practical in opposition to the theoretical. Others, particularly researchers in adult and continuing education, carried on decades-long arguments over whether quantitative research was more important than qualitative research. Still others squabbled over the importance of postmodernistic versus modernistic thought.

In the political world, people abandoned all tenets of conservative thought in favor of a liberal position (or vice versa). Adult educators who read the concepts of Malcolm Knowles (1980) learned that andragogy, at least as originally conceived in this country, was discussed in opposition to pedagogy—teaching adults versus teaching children.

The emphasis was always on the *versus*. Lines were drawn in the sand, and people chose sides. "Whose side are you on?" was often a battle cry, with fingers pointed at those who hadn't made up their minds.

The leadership literature is filled with dichotomies as well. Leadership is a transaction or a transformation (see Chapter Four). Leadership requires scientific data and careful rational analysis, or leadership should be regarded as an art and leadership decision making as intuitive.

In the new perspective for adult education leadership, we are moving past either-or to both-and. We are recognizing the importance that every coin has two sides, and if we fail to consider both sides, we have profoundly erred. For instance, adult education leadership is often rational *and* intuitive, efficient *and* effective, and so on.

Robert Quinn (1988) suggests an approach for both-and thinking. "The first step is recognizing polarities. The second step is seeing the strength and the weaknesses in each of the polar perspectives. The third and most challenging step is not to affix to one or the other but to move to a metalevel that allows one to see the interpenetrations and inseparability of the two polarities. The third step takes us to a transformational logic. It allows for simultaneous integration and differentiation. The new vision integrates the previously contradictory elements and results in synergy. It is here that excellence occurs" (pp. 164–165). For instance, an adult education leader may collect qualitative and quantitative data about a situation and at the same time listen to an intuitive internal voice about what decision should be made.

All of the positions expressed in this discussion suggest duality and the transcendence of either-or positions.

Linear and Nonlinear Thought

An old way of thinking assumes that all thought and activity are linear. One starts doing something at a defined beginning and then proceeds, step by step, phase by phase, to some previously defined completion point. Traditional adult education program planning is linear, if modeled on planning as in the textbooks. The preparation of adult education practitioners is generally viewed as a linear activity. Even a person's career is thought of as a linear progression, allowing for planning and preparation, and punctuated by clearly identified points to mark progress.

Conversely, some people have argued that all thought is non-linear and that linear thinking should be avoided entirely. For example, Frederick Hudson (1991) writes, "Our world has changed, but conventional wisdom has not. To make sense of adult life today, we need a fundamental change of consciousness, from linear to cyclical notions of how life works" (p. 30).

I don't go that far. I believe that the emerging age requires certain linear activities, some activities that are nonlinear, and many that are a combination of the two. At times, for instance, programmers must jump into projects not knowing whether they are at the beginning and not being too concerned. They attempt to respond to a problem but do not have time to do a systematic needs analysis and other preparatory work. They immediately begin programming for the problem. Jolie Solomon (1993), writing about a business application of this idea, says that we are moving toward ways of thinking and doing "mostly because the world moves faster and people (customers, voters) are more demanding. By the time the salesperson goes to ask her or his manager a question, the customer is in the store next door" (p. 44).

In some instances, a programmer may do some background study of a situation but then launch into a search for new directions in the midst of the program. The tendency, sometimes, is to try to plan for every contingency before moving forward. Too often these days, by the time such comprehensive planning is completed, the need for the program no longer exists.

Many activities in the emerging age do not move forward in sequence with a beginning, a middle, and an end. Most have peaks and valleys, movement forward and movement backward, circling back around and starting over again, lurching forward with huge gains and dropping back. Adult education administrators attempting to implement new organizational structures have experienced anything but a linear succession of activities. I am reminded of a university continuing education organization that was attempting an in-depth reorganization. The associate dean in charge of the effort had organized a series of meetings attended by faculty and middle managers. He was pleased with how everything was moving. One day he showed me the flowchart of his plan, which included a first set of meetings and a second set, followed by a written plan submitted to everyone for approval. According to the flowchart, the plan was then ready to be put into effect.

A month or two later I saw this administrator and asked him how the reorganization was coming. "It's not," he said. He went on to explain that a group of "saboteurs" (his word) had completely sidetracked the process. "I was blindsided," he confided. "Now I'm starting all over again."

What happened to this administrator is of course not new; it merely underlines how the best-laid linear plans can turn chaotic and unpredictable.

Some activities, like life itself, have cyclic characteristics, returning to the same themes again and again. Hudson (1991) says, "Cyclical implies going in circles, with the repetition of familiar patterns—night and day, the four seasons, birth and death. From this perspective, the purpose of life is to master the repetitive patterns in our ever-changing experience. Cyclical thinking looks for human meaning in the ongoing flow of daily experience, from world news to family events to personal concerns. It assumes that life can make sense in good times and in bad, in growth and decline, in beginnings and endings. Cyclical thinking tolerates high levels of ambiguity and finds pathways for living in dark and unseemly places, if necessary" (pp. 30–31).

James Gleick (1987) argues that there are far more nonlinear systems than many people are willing to accept, situations where straight lines and forward movement are not givens. "Nonlinear systems generally cannot be solved and cannot be added together.

In fluid systems and mechanical systems, the nonlinear terms tend to be the features that people want to leave out when they try to get a good, simple understanding" (pp. 23–24).

Finally, the Spanish philosopher José Ortega y Gasset (1960) talks about an alternative to linear thinking when he describes how he writes: "My proposal [is] not to follow a straight line but to develop my thoughts in successive circles of a shortening radius, hence in a spiral curve. This allows us, indeed obliges us, to present each question first in a form which is most popular, least rigorous but most understandable, certain that we will find it treated later with more energy and more formality in a narrower circle" (p. 71).

Adult education leaders facing the emerging age and trying to articulate the new perspective on adult education will often benefit by combining elements of linear and nonlinear thought. We are clearly moving from a world where machines were the metaphor and predictability the expectation, to a much more unpredictable world that moves more in cycles than in straight lines and has more characteristics of living organisms than of machines.

Growing and Sustaining

Remember the old assumptions? Unless an adult education organization is increasing in size, more students are enrolled, and more money is taken in, the organization is ineffective. If adult education administrators' budgets do not show an increase from year to year, the program is not successful. For many years this country's thinking has been growth oriented—how to achieve it, organize for it, and adjust to it. But it is increasingly outdated to assume that becoming ever larger is always good. Examples of the results of rampant growth are the restructuring problems such firms as IBM, General Motors, and General Dynamics have faced.

Mitroff (1988, p. 130) cites several instances where more actually results in less. When more money is spent on controlling crime, less money is available for preventing crime. When new roads are built to overcome traffic congestion, more congestion occurs because the new roads attract more traffic.

A few years ago, in an adult education organization where I worked, the request came for more evaluation and more accountability for funds spent. The organization took the challenge to heart, hiring a team of evaluators and asking everyone to write evaluation stories, be a part of evaluation surveys, and take time to have their units "externally evaluated." For six months, programming nearly ground to a halt as everyone tried to be more accountable. More attention to accountability resulted in less programming, with some lingering bad attitudes about evaluation and accountability that plague the organization to this day.

The emerging way of thinking does not always assume that more is better, though sometimes that may be the case. Emerging thinking considers *sustaining* a companion to *growing*. For organizations, rather than becoming ever larger, sustaining means creating a size that allows for effective work, optimal human interaction, and appropriate handling of environmental, economic, and human concerns.

A challenge that all adult education leaders face is knowing when to seek growth and when to realize that small or medium size may be better than large. Growth continues as an important guide in many situations, but in many other situations it is an obsolete concept. The paradox is for leaders to be able to work at both growing and sustaining.

Mitroff (1988) argues for the difference between growth and development (sustaining). He says that growth is usually measured in quantitative terms but development is reflected in qualitative factors. Growth is based on the assumption that bigger is better; development, on the assumption that less is more. "Cemeteries grow each year, but they don't develop" (p. 132).

Note that sustaining does not mean keeping alive programs or organizations that have served their purpose or have not worked. Such programs ought to be encouraged and even assisted to die.

A sustaining organization is vibrant and valuable; for such an organization, growth may have more negative than positive consequences.

Approaches and Goals

In the old way of thinking, the destination was more important than the journey. How you got to a goal or a destination was irrelevant; what counted was that you got there. The emerging way of thinking suggests a <u>balance between how you do something (approaches) and the outcomes (goals)</u>.

The adult education leader constantly faces choices between approaches and goals. For example, a continuing education dean recently shared with me the agony he faced in deciding how to fire a department head who was highly proficient in the technical aspects of her work but alienated nearly everyone with whom she had contact. After an extended effort to assist this department head, the decision was finally made to let her go. Now the question became how to do it. Firing someone is never easy. One way to do it, of course, is to send the person a letter and lay out the decision and the reasons for it. The job is done, the goal is met.

In this instance the dean met with the person for an extended length of time, helping her understand the reasons for her firing, giving her a full year's notice to allow time to find other work, and asking if she would continue providing technical assistance where she was proficient. There was much more involved than this brief account would suggest, but the result was that the department head ultimately left without undue anger or feelings of rejection.

Contrast that case with the following situation, which was handled quite differently. It occurred at a firm with a large data analysis facility. While the dozen or so employees in the data analysis department were attending a meeting to look at future directions for their unit, they received notices to return to the home city and meet at a nearby hotel. At the hotel meeting, they were handed letters telling them that they were fired and that they would be accompanied to their locked offices to pick up their personal belongings. That was it. The fired employees' anger and bitterness continue to this day.

When we begin talking about a balance between approaches and goals, we enter the realm of ethics. We can ask several questions: Are certain approaches to leadership more ethical than others? By what criteria do we determine which approaches are ethical and which are not? Henry A. Giroux (1992) writes, "Ethics . . . is not a matter of individual choice or relativism but a social discourse that refuses to accept needless human suffering and exploitation. Ethics becomes a practice that broadly connotes one's personal and social sense of responsibility to [others]. Thus, ethics is taken up as a struggle against inequality and as a discourse for expanding basic human rights" (p. 74). From a practical perspective, Giroux challenges all of us to look at what we do and how we do it from an ethical perspective.

There are further questions we could ask: How do we keep a goal in sight and at the same time pay attention to the approaches for reaching it? What is an appropriate balance for attending to approaches and goals? And, in the broader view, how do we attend to the paradox of both attending to the details of the journey and at the same time keeping our eye on the destination—attending to the approaches we use in leading and conducting educational events and attending to the intended outcomes? And at still another level, how do we allow for the interplay of approaches and goals? How do the approaches we use to reach a given goal influence the goal, and how does the identification of a sought-for goal influence the approaches we will use? The emerging age requires that we all wrestle, perhaps more than we have in the past, with the relationship of approaches and goals.

Competition and Cooperation

When I worked for the Cooperative Extension Service, I recall the many conversations we had about our competitors, the vocational schools. "Be careful about what information you share with them," colleagues warned me, implying that they steal information for their programs. Another time we were asked to cooperate with the state Department of Agriculture on an educational program. Most of the conversation was about who would get credit for the work, not what the nature of the programs would be. So much for interinstitutional cooperation!

Competition as the driving force for all human activity is an old way of thinking, part of the old perspective. As a result of competition, there are winners and losers. It was incomprehensible that in many situations, everyone might be a winner.

The new perspective suggests combinations of competition and cooperation, approaches that blend the two in such a way that we cannot tell where one begins and the other ends, and the result is something more than either. For adult learning organizations, a useful place to start is the relationship of adult learning organizations to one another. How can we assist each other so that the results surpass what could be accomplished through mere cooperation or competition?

Efficiency and Effectiveness

In the old perspective, efficiency sits on a pedestal. Efficiency is accepted as a high-level value, sought for and fought for but never questioned. Doing more, ever faster, and with fewer resources is a guiding principle for many businesses. Increasingly, efficiency has become a guiding principle for educational organizations as well. But in too many instances it is wrong to believe that every situation can be considered from the standpoint of efficiency.

A balancing term is effectiveness. The new way of thinking examines the relationship of activities from perspectives that often include efficiency but go well beyond it. Recently, I worked with a group of adult education leaders studying the history of civil rights and the black experience in central Alabama. It would have been efficient to focus on reading and lectures about these topics. But we also lived with black families in central Alabama. We visited civil rights sites and talked with people who participated in the marches and the protests. Our organization of the experience was far from efficient, but it was extremely effective.

Specialization and Generalization

Specialization has become a shibboleth in education. The old perspective embraces the assumption that because the world is becoming increasingly complex, people must specialize to succeed. But there are serious doubts as to whether this tilt toward specialization is appropriate. Needed also are people who can see across disciplines and make connections, who can discern broader contexts and multiple problems—true generalists. An emerging way of thinking (really a return to an older way) recognizes that our society needs both specialists and generalists.

Many adult education leaders come out of narrow discipline areas. They may be historians, sociologists, or agronomists, but when they become administrators, they must learn how to think across, between, and outside disciplines as well. Not long ago, the chairman of the agronomy department at a western university was appointed associate dean. I talked with him several months later about his new position.

"The biggest problem I had at first," he confided, "was to quit thinking like an agronomist and begin thinking more broadly. And that is not an easy task." He went on to tell me that he knew his agronomy discipline well, but when people from other disciplines began talking, he felt he needed to know their disciplines in order to be effective. After several months of frustration, he said, it finally dawned on him that his job was much more than knowing what was going on in the various disciplines at the university. Related to issues of specialization and generalization is the relationship of parts to wholes.

Parts and Wholes

Under the influence of a narrow view of scientific thought, it was believed that to study something, one had to examine its component parts. This reductionistic approach to research and thinking assisted in the development of specializations, but it often obscured larger views. Another fundamental flaw in the reductionistic approach is the belief that after studying the various components of a situation and adding the results together, one would have a view of the whole. Logically, this made sense, but practically, it failed. The old cliché of not being able to see the forest for the trees is a good example. One can study each tree in a forest in great depth and yet not have a view of the interrelation of trees or any sense of the totality of the forest that transcends the individual trees.

Similar thinking applies to leadership. As leaders, we can analyze situations deeply, taking them apart and scrutinizing each piece. Then we can add them back together and fool ourselves into believing that we are looking at the whole picture. Adult education leaders are aware of many examples of this. There was a time when potential employees were given batteries of tests in an attempt to determine their personality type, their emotional stability, their likelihood of getting along with people, and a host of other factors. But intangibles that transcended all these tests often made the difference in whether the person fit into the organization. The various tests were indicators; they were helpful but not sufficient.

Similar thinking applies to examining communities with the intent of providing programming information. One can examine a community from several traditional perspectives—social, political, economic, cultural—and still miss capturing the essence or the spirit of the community. Such views are obtained only by viewing the community as a whole, rather than attempting to add up the findings of various microstudies, valuable as they might be. The point often missed is that adding up the results of such microstudies does not describe the community; it merely compounds the foci of the studies.

Individuals and society are influenced by the world around them, and vice versa. Fritjof Capra ([1975] 1991), a physicist, said it well when he wrote, "The further we penetrate into the submicroscopic world, the more we shall realize how the modern physicist, like the Eastern mystic, has come to see the world as a system of inseparable, interacting, and ever-moving components, with man as an integral part of this system" (p. 11). What this means is that no person, organization, community, or state can operate in isolation, no matter how hard it tries, and hence as adult education leaders we are compelled to examine wholes as well as parts. *"For whom the Bell Tolls" John Donne 1700s*

Scientific Knowledge and Knowledge from Other Sources

The old perspective values knowledge that is rational and scientifically based more highly than knowledge derived by other means. Such rational and scientifically based knowledge is often considered to be the "right" knowledge.

An emerging view is that knowledge is multifaceted and comes from many sources. Some knowledge is scientific; it comes from carefully designed and conducted experiments or well-monitored surveys and interviews. Other knowledge is the knowledge of elders, their wisdom coming from years of thought and action. Also included is the artist's knowledge that bursts forth in swatches of color on a canvas, reverberating sound in a concert hall, or compelling, heart-wrenching stories that leap from the printed page.

Jim Dawson (1992) writes, "The failure of traditional Western science to recognize Indian science, in large part, is due to the vastly different ways the cultures view the world. Native Americans tie their science to a larger view of the world, including the spiritual, while Western scientists demand objectivity and compartmentalization of details." Quoting Thom Alcoz, a Cherokee Indian and academic biologist, Dawson points out that Western textbooks explain that humans breathe out carbon dioxide and inhale oxygen, while trees do the reverse through photosynthesis, and label each segment of the process. Native Americans are likely to say, "We share our breath with the trees." Knowledge from different cultures takes on different forms, but that does not make knowledge from one culture more "right" or "appropriate" than knowledge from another culture.

Not to be overlooked is the knowledge of the people—indigenous knowledge, the knowledge that comes from people's lives of struggle and survival. This knowledge reflects joy and sorrow, success and failure. It is real and powerful knowledge and is often overlooked by the merchants who create and sell knowledge in the marketplace.

Likewise, the sources of knowledge for the adult education leader are many and varied, just as our examples suggest. In the new perspective on adult education leadership, no longer can a leader remain tied only to scientific evidence. Leaders for the emerging age will be individuals who can draw successfully from many sources, including their own indigenous knowledge.

Consistency and Paradox

Adult education leaders prefer consistency in their lives. They like to know that when they sit behind their desk in the morning, what they expected to do is what they end up doing. Yet more often than not, they face situations that initially make no sense. They are paradoxes, ideas in conflict. Paradox involves inconsistency and ambiguity, two or more positions that each sound reasonable yet conflict or even contradict each other.

We live in a paradoxical time, not unlike what Charles Dickens ([1859] 1950) wrote in *A Tale of Two Cities*: "It was the best of times, it was the worst of times, it was the age of wisdom, it was the age of foolishness, it was the epoch of belief, it was the epoch of incredulity, it was the season of Light, it was the season of Darkness, it was the spring of hope, it was the winter of despair, we had everything before us, we had nothing before us . . ." (p. 3).

Paradox is everywhere these days. Advancements in technology, as noted earlier, have resulted in extraordinary achievements. Yet the cities of the world face the constant threat of riots. Infrastructures in many nations, particularly the United States, continue to deteriorate, resulting in power outages, transportation shutdowns, and air that is often dangerous to breathe.

A common paradox in adult education is administrators' being asked to do more programming but losing program support staff due to budget cuts. Without the support staff, programmers cannot keep programming even at previous levels.

Walter Anderson (1990, pp. 243–250) discusses paradox in another way. He says that six sets of what I call competing belief systems are operating in the world and that they are increasingly coming into contact and conflict. Paraphrasing Anderson, the six belief sets are these:

1. *The technology, economic development, and progress view*. This is a common view in the United States, held by both major political parties, accepted by most colleges and universities, and accepted without question by many people as a core belief for the Western world. The logic is this: technology leads to economic development, which in turn leads to progress.

2. *The ecological or sustainable view*. People who subscribe to this view reject progress as myth and challenge technology and economic development strategies. This view is promoted by the Greens, a serious political movement in many countries of the

world. It is also a view, I would argue, of several environmental groups in this country.

Me 3. *The Christian fundamentalist view.* People who hold this view want to see a return to a society that is governed on the basis of Christian values and biblical belief. A society's values have an absolute foundation and authority according to this view. There appears to be a growing interest in this belief in the United States.

4. *The Islamic fundamentalist view.* People advocating this view want a return to basic Islamic values and koranic belief.

Avis 5. *The Socialist-Marxist view.* In recent years a severe challenge has been launched against this view in Eastern Europe and in the former Soviet Union. But it still continues in many parts of the world and has many staunch believers.

Jeri 6. *The new paradigm view.* People with this view—and their numbers are growing—favor a new approach that relegates old ones, like those on this list, to the past. This new world view takes a global perspective. These people believe that paradigm change—a shifting of perspectives—is necessary for us to move toward a global community.

Anderson (1990) goes to some length to describe each of these societal directions, providing examples of where they are occurring and have recently occurred in the world. He also makes the point that each perspective has its strong adherents somewhere. Consequently, according to Anderson, a variety of perspectives exist in the world. Proponents of each believe that they are correct and in most instances feel that it is their mission to show people who believe differently the error of their ways. Clearly, the world is in the midst of an ideological paradox.

Peter Vaill (1989) says we are also experiencing a "grand paradox of management" (p. 77). He says the paradox of management is the contradiction between more than fifty years of teaching rational organizational analysis, design, and control of human systems and organizations that continue to be "mysterious, recalcitrant, intractable, unpredictable, paradoxical, absurd, and—unless it's your own ox getting gored—funny" (p. 77).

Still another paradox is the long-standing conflict between art and science or between the intuitive and the rational. The artist often dismisses the scientist as overly concerned with rationality, control, and linear thought. The scientist dismisses artistic work as intuitive, subjective, unverifiable thought resulting in impractical outcomes.

So the current era is one of paradox at several levels. We see paradox as we confront unpredictable and multifaceted global political and economic systems. And we increasingly see paradox within the organizations that we are asked to manage and lead.

Scientific Values and Beliefs, Personal Values and Beliefs

In the old perspective, leaders relied heavily on beliefs and values based on science and rational thought for their decision making. In the new perspective, adult education leaders also rely on their personal values and beliefs. Understanding one's values and beliefs is key to dealing with an ever-changing and unpredictable society. In Chapters Five and Six I discuss in some depth an approach for uncovering personal values and beliefs and examining them in light of contemporary situations.

Some people argue that what is needed in these times of chaotic change is a return to basic values and beliefs. Translated, this often means a return to some set of values and beliefs from the past. I would agree that some values and beliefs may have the power to transcend time as well as geography and culture. But many values and beliefs do not. For instance, I grew up valuing working long hours. It took me many years to realize that merely working long hours did not guarantee greater productivity. I've now modified this value to incorporate the concept of working smarter rather than working longer. Resurrecting old values is not what I am suggesting here. What is important for the emerging age is that leaders have a foundation, an examined core of beliefs and values, that guides them during times of paradox, ambiguity, and chaotic change.

Predictable and Nonpredictable Change

The old way of thinking assumes that change is the only constant in a rapidly changing world. The emerging way of thinking assumes that change itself is changing. A predominant characteristic of the emerging age is the nature of change. At various times in the history of the world, change has ranged from mild and predictable, sometimes even incremental, to chaotic and catastrophic. For instance, moving from hundreds of years of human and animal power to machine power was a dramatic change. After the first machines appeared (steam engines, for example) machine power quickly moved from internal combustion engines to electrical motors to nuclear-powered engines. These changes influenced all dimensions of human life—personal, social, economic, and political. But perhaps most important, these changes affected how human beings saw themselves and the world.

Over the centuries, vast shifts have occurred in political structures as some countries moved from dictatorship to socialism to democracy and then often back to dictatorship. Centuries of war brought changes affecting millions of people and causing great upheaval. Hundreds of additional examples could be cited; the point is that change is not a foreign concept to human beings.

Change is, of course, a driver for the emerging age, and as mentioned, not only has it become more rapid, but the nature of change itself has changed. Charles Handy (1989) calls this new change "discontinuous." He contrasts continuous (predictable) and discontinuous (nonpredictable) change and points out that "continuous change is comfortable change. The past is . . . the guide to the future" (p. 3). By contrast, Handy explains that discontinuous change often has little or no relationship to the past. It occurs unexpectedly and is not part of a pattern. Examples of discontinuous change in recent history include the dissolution of the Soviet Union and the demolition of the Berlin Wall. No one predicted either event; neither was part of a pattern. An important characteristic of discontinuous change is unpredictability. Peter Vaill (1989) calls this chaotic change. He uses the metaphor of permanent white water to describe the situation in which much of the world finds itself these days. It is a time that Harrison Owen (1991) described as riding a tiger. From my perspective, adult education leaders are on the tiger's back, and the animal is charging through the underbrush. We don't know how to steer the tiger anymore, and we have no idea where it is going, if indeed it has a destination in mind. We fear jumping or falling off the tiger, for in the jungle may lurk dangers far greater than those we are experiencing on the tiger's back. If we jump off, the tiger itself might devour us. So we struggle to hold on as the tiger bounds over muddy terrain and gallops through underbrush that tears at our clothes.

Srivastva, Cooperrider, and Associates (1990) put it this way: "The meaning of everything is under assault in this chaotic world" (p. 2). I think of it as a time of stormy weather. As I was growing up, on a farm in central Wisconsin, storms were a part of my family's life, as they are for all farmers. Summer storms blew up quickly. Some were violent, with crashing thunder and sky-splitting lightning. Other storms were more inconvenient than they were dangerous, stopping our planned work and causing us to make unplanned adjustments in our daily activities.

Stormy weather is a metaphor for the age we are now entering. Much of today's change cannot be predicted. We have no blueprints or recipes that tell us what to do if X or Y or Z occurs. Seldom can we anticipate the effects of a particular change, just as we cannot anticipate the effects of a storm. Even during stormy weather, there are moments of calm, when the sun comes out and the wind quits blowing and the ominous clouds disappear over the horizon. Sometimes, in these periods of calm, we are lulled into believing that severe storms are a part of history and that we shouldn't be concerned. We go about our business and then are devastated when the next storm strikes.

If we use stormy weather as a metaphor for change in our society, we might note that the periods of calm between storms have become shorter and shorter, so we have less and less time to become complacent. In the succession of storms, some are severe and some less so. Some storms feature wicked lightning, others have strong winds, and still others leave the landscape buried in snow. After a storm, we try to assess the damage, pick ourselves up, and move on. Too often we are so overcome by the negatives of a storm that we overlook the positives. It is possible that what at first might appear as a horrendous negative turns out to be a great positive—if we are open enough to recognize it. As blasphemous as this may sound to some, the rounds of budget cuts and freezes that many adult education organizations have faced in the past several years have forced a reexamination of mission and direction, the development of vision, and the exploration of new structures as well as new approaches to leading. When everything is going well, few people listen to calls for change. On the positive side, the recent rounds of budget cuts and restructuring have awakened the sleeping giant that is adult education.

Both discontinuous and continuous change challenges adult education organizations and their leaders at every turn. In the next chapter I will explore several of these challenges in greater depth.

Chapter Three

Leadership
Then and Now

New kinds of leaders will emerge to lead in ways different from those that we have known in the past. As J. Cole (1992) says, "Different times and different conditions demand different approaches—and usually the harder the times, the more radical the approach" (p. 18). Charles Handy (1989) affirms this position when he writes, "Discontinuous change requires discontinuous upside-down thinking to deal with it, even if both thinker and thoughts appear absurd at first sight" (p. 5).

Change swirls around adult education organizations and their leaders these days, and the changes are likely to increase in intensity and complexity. There are new demands, new pressures, and new expectations for adult education organizations and their leaders. It is a time when all of society's leaders face problems and challenges, and often they have to develop strategies for dealing with them as they face them. Handy (1989) goes on to say, "We may all need new rules for new ball games and will have to discover them for ourselves" (p. 9).

"I'm facing problems these days that didn't exist five years ago," one continuing education dean said recently. She went on to tell me about her university's budget problems and the fact that she had to cut staff yet retain as many programs as possible. It was clear that she was agonizing over the personnel cuts, and she was frustrated by the prospect of responding with severely reduced resources to the many requests received each day.

At a national meeting, I sat with several cooperative extension directors who were discussing problems they had recently encountered. One of them said, "In the old days, five or six years ago, we took research results from the college researcher and gave them to people who applied the research. We knew how to do that, and we did it well."

I could see heads nodding in the group. The director went on. "You all know about BST, the biotechnology that can increase a dairy cow's capacity to produce milk." The expression on the faces of directors from dairy states suggested they knew where the discussion was going.

"When that technology came out and we began talking about it with farmers, BST became an issue. It was much more than merely a technology for helping farmers increase the production of their dairy cows. Community representatives said BST was one more technology to drive smaller farmers off the land and destroy small community organizations. People concerned about animal care responded with concerns about the welfare of animals and how BST would affect them. Persons concerned about human health raised questions about the safety of BST and whether it would contaminate milk. And on and on. As a director, people call me everyday with these questions, and I don't know which way to turn. It's a mess." The group agreed and went on to say that BST was likely just one of many such issues emerging as researchers continue to discover and create new and often controversial knowledge.

An administrator in a national nonprofit adult education organization told me that his organization had just gone through a major reorganization and a sharpening of focus and direction. The old organizational pattern wasn't working anymore, he said. He also shared some of the pain involved in making structural and organizational shifts, including some staff leaving and new staff joining the organization.

Recently, as part of a workshop I was offering for middle managers in an adult education organization, I was talking about new approaches for leadership and how leaders must learn to take control of their work and their lives. A young man in the front row, who had been in a middle-management position for about a year, challenged me. He said, "What you are saying sounds good, but let's be realistic. I have no control over my work whatever and little control over the rest of my life either. Someone is always demanding that I do this or that. It's all I can do to keep my head above water."

Several other people agreed with the speaker. The times have become terribly hard to control, with demands coming from supervisors, from subordinates, and from the public—from every direction. These adult education administrators are not alone; leaders everywhere face such problems at ever-increasing rates.

Many adult education organizations, operated for profit or not, are changing in ways that many people have difficulty comprehending. New kinds of adult education organizations are emerging. For example, I recently learned of a woman who, upon completing her graduate work, organized a for-profit adult education business. She immediately set out on her own and didn't even attempt to seek employment in a more traditional adult education organization such as a university extension. Whether she will succeed remains to be seen, but this woman is an example of the types of changes we are seeing.

Dray Wagons and Model T's

Change is difficult—for organizations and for people. It has always been and will likely continue to be so. We could compare some adult education organizations with dray wagons and their drivers. Dray wagons were familiar vehicles in every town throughout the country in the late 1800s and early 1900s, before automobiles and trucks. Pulled by a team of draft horses, dray wagons met each steam-driven train that rolled into town. They hauled supplies from the railroad depot to the various town businesses. In their day they were terribly important; indeed, they were vital links between the railroad and the customer.

After the Ford Model T truck appeared on the scene and provided more dependable transportation (though wintertime service in the northern states could be somewhat iffy), some
attempts were made to keep the dray wagons. The wagon owners
claimed they provided better service than the smelly, noisy little
trucks and urged their drivers to be more courteous and more reliable than ever before. For a time, the motorized truck and the
dray wagon coexisted—but not for long. Soon the dray wagons
disappeared. Some dray wagon operators evolved into trucking
companies. The trucks and their drivers continued to meet the
now diesel-powered trains and deliver goods from the depot to
the business establishments.

But then, in thousands of communities across the country, the
trains stopped running. The former dray wagon companies, now
trucking companies, faced yet another, even more formidable challenge: there was nothing to haul from the depot to the town's
places of business—in fact, there was no more depot. A few dray
companies became cross-country trucking companies, shifting from
relatively small trucks to huge long-haul behemoths. There was still
a great need to haul products from one place to another, but great
changes had to be made, and drivers and managers of trucking
companies needed skills far different from those required for managing a livery stable filled with draft horses and keeping the wagon's
wheels greased.

Many adult organizations continue to operate as if they were
dray wagons pulled by a team of high-stepping horses, with harness
bells ringing and the shod hooves clip-clopping along the cobble-
stone streets. Perhaps we need a few dray wagon adult education
organizations. But in most instances we need organizations that
provide transportation appropriate to the times in which we live.
Nostalgia may suggest that the adult education organizations we
have had, and the approach to leadership that worked for years,
will continue to serve well into the future. Some people erroneously

call this a return to basics. It is not a return to basics. It is a failure to face the reality of the times. Most adult learners will not climb aboard a dray wagon organization. They have neither the time nor the inclination nor the patience for such outdated educational approaches.

What are the characteristics of a dray wagon organization? Such an organization believes that change is for someone else. It programs as it has programmed, remains organized as it has been organized, and attempts to serve the audience it has always served. I know of a midwestern university that has successfully enrolled large numbers of adults in its degree programs. Courses were offered in the evening and on weekends. In contrast to attending classes during the day, several times a week, this alternative degree program was well received. But now participants in the program are asking for more. Participants want at least some of the courses offered at a distance, using computers or other educational technology so that they do not have to drive to campus. They want the flexibility of taking courses when the times are convenient for them. Participants want at least some of their coursework in a format that allows them the freedom to interact with the material in the evening, in the early morning, or at other times that the university may not find convenient. They want credit for activities they do in their jobs that relate to the subject matter they are studying. And so on.

The university argues against these changes. Administrators believe that such changes will "water down" the quality of their programs. So they continue offering programs as they have in the past, trying to be the best dray wagon organization possible. But they have discovered that fewer and fewer adult students want the university's program, particularly in the fashion that it is offered. They face a dilemma: do they continue as the best possible dray wagon organization, or do they attempt to make some fairly dramatic changes?

dated

Historical and Contemporary
Leadership Perspectives

Before examining the specific dimensions of a new leadership approach to adult education, let us briefly examine several of the leadership perspectives that provide a backdrop.

In the 1960s I conducted a research project that focused on three approaches to leadership: democratic, authoritarian, and laissez-faire. Simply put, democratic leaders involved people in decision making, authoritarian leaders made all the decisions themselves, and laissez-faire leaders did little of anything, allowing situations to play themselves out.

There was much talk in those days about which leadership approach was the best one for certain situations. For instance, in the military, authoritarian leadership was said to be the only way; in a university, democratic leadership was more likely appropriate; and so on. Few people seemed to agree that laissez-faire leadership was ever appropriate, yet many people could identify leaders they knew who followed that approach.

Other leadership theories were discussed at that time as well. *Trait theory* was a popular one. Leaders, whatever approach they used, were successful because of certain personal traits such as tone of voice, physical presence, or intelligence. Some of these traits could be developed, but many were the happenstance of birth. According to this theory, leaders were born. Their success was largely due to the traits they possessed and not so much to the approaches they used. (Haiman, 1951; Pigors, 1935; Ross and Hendry, 1957; Cartwright and Zander, 1953; Tead, 1935; and Lewin and Lippitt, 1937–1938, discuss various historical approaches to leadership.)

The *situational approach* argued that leaders were successful because the approach they used matched the situations in which they found themselves. Different situations demanded different kinds of leaders. Following the situational approach, some experts

experts argued that certain people were simply "not cut out" to lead in certain situations and hence should be steered away from them. Many attempts were made to match the person to the situation—often assuming that both the person and the situation were static.

Another approach that has attracted considerable attention in the past several years is the *transactional approach*. James Burns (1978) discusses various dimensions of transactional leadership in his Pulitzer Prize–winning book, *Leadership*. He states that transactional leadership occurs "when one person takes the initiative in making contact with others for the purpose of an exchange of valued things" (p. 19). In essence, to put it perhaps too succinctly, the transactional approach is based on a social exchange. The leader gains in prominence and status while helping the organization (followers) gain. There is a transaction. Leaders give and leaders gain, followers give and followers gain. Leaders influence those who follow, and vice versa.

Still another theory that has emerged recently is known as *transformational leadership*. Burns (1978) writes that transformational leadership occurs "when one or more persons engage with others in such a way that leaders and followers raise one another to higher levels of motivation and morality. . . . Their purposes, which might have started out as separate but related, as in the case of transactional leadership, become fused" (p. 20). Bernard Bass (1990), comparing transactional and transformational leaders, writes, "Although both types of leaders sense the felt needs of their followers, it is the transformational leader who raises consciousness [about higher considerations] through articulation and role modeling" (pp. 23–24). Bass also argues the possibility of combining elements of transactional and transformation leadership rather than putting them on opposite ends of a continuum, as he believes Burns does. Bass writes, "Many of the great transformational leaders, including Abraham Lincoln, Franklin Delano Roosevelt, and John F. Kennedy, did not shy away from being transactional as well as transformational" (p. 53).

Others, myself included, have taken a broader and somewhat different view of transformational leadership, building on Burns's and Bass's work but going beyond it. For example, Noel Tichy and Mary Anne Devanna (1986) have devoted an entire book to a discussion of the transformational leader. Their work builds on William Bridges's (1991) ideas about transitions and how individuals and organizations experience them in the process of change.

Not only has the concept of transformation gained prominence in leadership, but adult education practitioners and researchers have also given it considerable attention in the past several years. (I discuss transformation, particularly as it relates to leadership, in Chapter Eleven.)

Stephen Covey (1991, pp. 176–179) describes four "management paradigms" that could be called leadership theories:

1. *Scientific management* views people primarily as economic beings. The manager says, in relation to the people managed, "My task as a manager is to motivate them through . . . the carrot and the stick" (p. 176). "The management style [is] authoritarian. . . . An authoritarian manager makes the decision and gives the commands, the workers conform and cooperate, perform and contribute, as requested to receive the economic rewards of pay and other benefits" (p. 177).

2. In the *human relations paradigm,* the manager recognizes that in addition to being an economic necessity, people have feelings. "Hence we treat people not only with fairness, but with kindness, courtesy, civility, and decency. But it may only mean a shift from being an authoritarian to being a benevolent authoritarian because we still are the elite few who know what's best" (p. 177).

3. Following the *human resource paradigm,* "we work not only

with fairness and kindness, but also with efficiency. . . . With this larger understanding of [human] nature, we begin to make better use of [people's] talent, creativity, resourcefulness, ingenuity, and imagination. We begin to delegate more, realizing that people will do what's necessary to do if they're committed to a particular goal. We begin to see people as the main resource: not capital assets, not physical properties, but people—their hearts and minds" (p. 178).

4. With *principle-centered leadership*, "we work with fairness, kindness, efficiency, and effectiveness. We work with the whole person. We see that people are not just resources or assets, not just economic, social, and psychological beings. They are also spiritual beings; they want meaning, a sense of doing something that matters. People do not want to work for a cause with little meaning, even though it taps their mental capacities to the fullest. There must be purposes that lift them, ennoble them, and bring them to their highest selves" (pp. 178–179).

For the past several years, business and industry have confronted the need to develop new kinds of leaders and new approaches to leadership. Many studies have been conducted and several books written that show the direction for a new kind of leader and a new approach to leadership, among them Bennis (1989), Bolman and Deal (1991), Covey (1989, 1991), De Pree (1989, 1992), Drucker (1992), Gardner (1990), Handy (1989), Heider (1985), Koestenbaum (1991), Kotter (1990), Kouzes and Posner (1990), Mitroff (1988), Nanus (1989, 1990, 1992), Peters (1987), Quinn (1988), Senge (1990), Tichy and Devanna (1986), Vaill (1989), and Wheatley (1992).

The new perspective on adult education leadership builds on many of these theories and approaches. Certain leadership traits assist leaders, but with few exceptions these traits can be improved on if they are lacking. Leaders for the emerging age are people with confidence, courage, and vision. (See Chapter Six for a discussion of leader qualities and characteristics.) These are different from such traits as physical stature and timber of voice, often mentioned in the historical literature on leadership traits.

Leaders must be concerned with situations (contexts) but not totally caught up in them. Different leadership approaches are encouraged for different situations, but that does not mean that leaders are dictated to solely by the context in which they work. Concern for context does not suggest that contexts can be categorized and matched with the most effective leadership approaches that may be applied. Increasingly, leaders develop approaches that are unique to the contexts in which they work.

In many instances there is an exchange, a transaction. Leaders and organizations gain. But in most instances, the basis for leadership is more subtle and profound than a mere social exchange. Commitment, dedication, and sharing in the making of an organizational vision require more than simply a social exchange, a transaction—although an exchange is certainly part of the process.

As I will discuss later, in many instances leadership effort results in a transformation, a profound change in leaders and followers, and in organizations, agencies, and institutions. The nature of this transformation may actually change the lives of the individuals involved. People leave behind old ways of thinking and acting; organizations build different structures and relationships and develop different procedures for carrying out their tasks.

Finally, leaders view people as whole persons, striving to provide situations in which people can find meaning and can express their spiritual as well as their mental potential.

Overcoming Myths

For a new perspective on adult education leadership to emerge, several myths about leadership must be confronted and overcome.

Myth 1: There Is No Such Thing as
Leadership Theory or the Study of Leadership

I asked interns in an intensive leadership development program I coordinated, in which the study of research and scholarship on leadership played an important part, to interview the head of the organization in which they worked. They were to ask questions about this administrator's approach to leadership and leadership development. In more than one instance, the head of an organization said, "There is no such thing as the study of leadership. If you're going to be the kind of tough leader we need today, you learn by working on the job. First and foremost, you must be a respected scholar in some area of expertise. The leadership business will take care of itself."

The interns were taken aback. Denying that leadership can be studied is not an unusual position. The stance is similar to saying that the sole determinant of success as a teacher is an in-depth knowledge of the subject matter.

Many leaders who deny the study of leadership have likely learned to reflect on their own actions and those of other successful leaders and drawn lessons from them. These are extremely important strategies for improving as a leader. However, they are usually not sufficient, given the enormous challenges leaders face these days and the value to be acquired from other people's experiences and perspectives captured in the research and scholarship of leadership development work.

Others have even been more extreme in their comments about leadership development. Benjamin De Mott (1993), a humanities professor, calls the study of leadership a cult, "a no-less-perfect specimen of late-twentieth-century academic avarice and a precise depth gauge of some recent professorial descents into pap, cant, and jargon" (p. 61).

Another view of this myth concerns the way people understand leadership development theory and process. Tom Sergiovanni, a

Trinity University professor, was asked if he believed leadership was an outdated concept. His response: "Not leadership; what's outdated is our understanding of it" (Brandt, 1992, p. 46). People like Sergiovanni discount much of the present and past theory and practice of educational leadership—a position often taken in this book as well.

Myth 2: After This Organizational Change, We Can Expect a Period of Calm

In the maelstrom of modern life, organizational change and renewal never stop. Looking forward to periods of "normalcy," when the organization is not changing, is an artifact of yesterday's thinking. As mentioned earlier, organizations must learn as well as teach. Just as everyone in an organization must be constantly learning and changing, so must the organization itself. The normal state for an organization is ongoing renewal and concomitant change.

In a continuing education organization where I once worked, we spent most of a year working out a new organizational arrangement. At one time or another nearly everyone in the organization had some role in making a decision about how this large organization should be structured, who should be reporting to whom, the number of middle managers, and so on. I was working in a staff and organization development position in those days and thus had responsibility for organizing much of the restructuring effort.

I have never forgotten a comment made by the administrative head of the organization to the entire faculty upon completion of the written plan. "Be assured," he said, "this is the last time we'll need to work on organizational change for a good long time."

Less than a year later, we were back making major organizational changes, trying to keep up with the ever-mutating context.

Myth 3: An Administrative Leader's Main Role Is to Keep the Organization, As It Now Exists, Operating Properly

In one of my leadership workshops, a top-level adult education administrator came up to me during a break. We had spent most of the morning talking about organizational development and renewal.

"I am more than a little disturbed," he began. "Why are you spending all this time talking about organizational change?"

"Say more," I replied.

"My job is to make this organization function as well as possible, to do what our mission says we are supposed to do, to keep our stakeholders happy, to make sure our staff is doing what it is supposed to do, to be accountable to those who provide the money."

"That's mostly right," I said.

"That's entirely right," he continued to argue. "It is none of my business to push this organization toward change. I've got my hands full making it operate the way it is now organized."

This administrative leader's position is not unique. Yet in my judgment, a major role for an adult education leader is to encourage, support, facilitate, and otherwise ensure that the organization continues to change. Administrative leaders who see their main role as preserving an organization as it has existed face enormous difficulties in chaotic times.

Myth 4: Leaders Lead and Followers Follow   *Wish it were true!*

Bolman and Deal (1991) call this the "heroic image" of leadership, wherein the process is viewed as one-way. They go on to say, "Such a view blinds us to the reality that leadership fundamentally involves a relationship between leaders and their constituents" (p. 409). Rather than a one-way process, leaders and constituents interact constantly, each influencing the other. Also, the heroic view of leadership prevents any leadership sharing, whereby everyone in an organization has responsibility for leadership. Following the heroic myth of leadership, the people in top positions have all the responsibility for leadership, which, in today's environment, makes the task impossible. Leaders who believe this myth are almost always doomed to fail.

Staff members who believe this myth expect more from their leaders than the leaders can humanly deliver. Such staffs may also develop dependent, even parent-child–type relationships with their leaders.

I know an adult education organization that operates on the premise that the administrative leaders are in charge of everything that happens in the organization. Although the organization has been able to hire extremely well-qualified staff members, these staffers are highly dependent on their supervisors for direction. Attending a meeting with several staffers recently, I heard such comments as "If only my supervisor would tell me more clearly what to do, I could get on with my work" and "When are they going to decide which way this organization is headed?"

In organizations that continue to follow this myth, the leadership potential in everyone who works there is never realized.

Myth 5: There Is No Difference Between Leadership and Management

Even though both leadership and management functions often occur simultaneously and may be performed by the same person, it is important to recognize the differences between the two. John Gardner (1990) says leaders, in contrast to managers, emphasize organizational renewal, stress the importance of vision, are able to see a world larger than their own organization, are able to think for the long as well as the short term, and have the capacity to deal with multiple constituencies and constantly changing conditions.

Examining metaphors may also reveal differences between leadership and management. Managers climb ladders, carefully, one step at a time; leaders are the ones who decide where the ladders are placed. Managers keep a ship running, the engine oiled, and everything in good repair, while leaders steer the ship and decide where it is headed. Leaders are also the designers of the ship; they decide the ship's size and characteristics and what it can and cannot do. The manager of a farm makes sure the crops are planted, cared for, and harvested on time. The leader decides which crops to plant and indeed whether any crops will be planted in a given year.

A common cliché tells us that managers do things right, leaders do the right things. Or as Covey (1989) says, "Management is a bottom line focus: How can I best accomplish certain things? Leadership deals with the top line: What are the things I want to accomplish?" (p. 101).

Leadership and management are closely related. As Bolman and Deal (1991) point out, "It is hard to imagine an outstanding manager who is not also a leader" (p. 408). An organization with outstanding leadership but with average or below-average management will experience severe difficulties and may fail. A well-managed organization with average or below-average leadership will continue for a time, but it too will fail. Both leadership and management are necessary in an organization. Unfortunately, there are more good managers today than there are good leaders. And there is also confusion that good management equals good leadership—that if the organization is properly managed, it is properly led.

I worked as consultant to an adult education organization recently where the administrative head was an excellent manager but had few of the important leadership qualities. She had reams of data about her organization. She knew the enrollment trends; she knew which courses and workshops had been successful over the past five years; she had budget data showing costs of instruction; her annual reports sparkled with detail. She knew what was going on and where. But she had no vision for the future of her organization. Her gaze was inward, not outward. The organization, even though it was well managed, was beginning to see enrollment decline. Her response was to ask for yet one more survey to gather additional data about current offerings rather than to begin a long-range vision-making process. In addition, she had always been uncomfortable representing her organization to the public and relating with other organizations in the community. What she liked best was managing the details of her operation. Unless this administrator starts to take on more leadership roles, the organization's future is bleak.

In many adult education organizations, leadership and management responsibilities fall to the same person. One moment they are managers; the next moment they are making leadership decisions. It is certainly possible, and usually desirable, for strong leaders to have competent management skills. It is also helpful for competent managers to have well-developed leadership skills.

In recent years, adult education administrative leaders have greatly increased their competency in managing adult education agencies, organizations, and institutions. Considerable research and scholarship have concentrated on helping adult education administrators develop proficiency in budgeting, planning, supervising, marketing, finding and organizing teaching resources, reporting, and evaluating (for example, see Beder, 1986; Boone, 1985; Boyle, 1981; Courtenay, 1990; Houle, 1972; Knox, 1982, 1990, 1991; Knox and Associates, 1980; Matkin, 1985; Patton, 1990; Simerly and Associates, 1987; Smith and Offerman, 1989; and Strother and Klus, 1982). Organizations such as the Learning Resources Network (LERN) in Manhattan, Kansas, and the College Board in New York City have offered workshops, conferences, seminars, video and audio tapes, books, and monographs on such topics as brochure development, marketing strategies, financial record keeping, and enrollment systems, all designed to make the management of adult education operations more systematic and effective.

With all the changes that are affecting adult education providers, even the best management is not enough. What will be required is exemplary management plus a new kind of leadership.

A New Kind of Leadership

The new perspective on leadership in adult education is an approach in process, is built on multiple foundations, and includes the development of leadership capacity.

An Approach in Process

The new perspective on adult education leadership in the emerging age is an approach that is constantly open to change and development and to adaptation based on the life history of the leader, the context in which the leader works, and the demands of particular leadership situations. The new perspective is an approach in process, subject to continuous change and adjustment. It is about shared leadership and cooperation, multiple perspectives and intuitive wisdom, developing a shared vision, and providing an environment where everyone in an organization knows where the organization is headed and believes in the vision.

Multiple Foundations

Adult education's new leadership perspective has its roots in the marriage of the arts, humanities, and sciences. It builds on the work of scientific researchers who have studied leadership. It also builds on the work of artists and philosophers who see the world in a different way. It brings together the rationality and focus of the scientist; the images, tales, and metaphors of the artist; a perspective on the past from the historian; and the philosopher's concern for broader questions such as the nature of reality and the place for ethics.

The new leader, in Peter Vaill's (1990) words, "is required to be able to reflect and philosophize to a degree that sometimes astonishes (and infuriates) the down-to-earth, no-nonsense, let's get-on-with-it sorts of men and women who have traditionally held these jobs" (p. 21). Vaill goes on to describe the new leader as an artist.

"The artist, of whatever sort, tends to possess extraordinary competency with respect to such things as the nature of his or her materials, the history of the particular art, the ways the artistic product is likely to be experienced by others, methods of working, and the like. But all of these unitary competencies are subordinate to something else: *the expressiveness of the artist*, whether we call this expressiveness 'creativity' or 'insight' or 'inspiration' or whatever. I define 'art' as the attempt to wrest coherence and meaning out of more reality than we ordinarily try to deal with" (p. 39).

The closest we can come to understanding the artistic dimension of leadership is listening to leaders' stories as they describe what they do and how they do it. From these stories we can obtain clues to the artistry of leadership practice. We can also observe outstanding leaders in action. But for many of us, it is difficult to see what they do that is clearly making a difference. Asking a leader to describe exactly what makes a difference in how he or she leads is comparable to asking a painter to describe the process of creating an artistic work. If the artist is patient, you might hear something about brushes and paint and perspective. The artist will tell you that skills and knowledge about brushes and paints are certainly necessary, but such knowledge and skills, even developed to a high level, still leave you a long way from being an artist.

Artists will tell you that it is difficult to describe what is most important about a creative work. The character of creative activity is also quite different from artist to artist. I want to stress this last point. We can certainly learn many skills and much knowledge about leading, but the artistry of leadership is a personal thing. Each of us is challenged to find our own leader's voice, which comes from within. A leader's voice is not pursued in the wild, captured, and made one's own. We are each obligated to develop our own voice.

I remember being part of a small group of people talking with a prominent nature artist, Owen Gromme. He was describing a painting of a ruffed grouse he had recently completed, with a background of fall leaves and a downed tree. Someone asked him about the kind of paint he used and how he mixed colors to achieve the wonderfully realistic feathers of the grouse. Someone else asked him how he prepared the canvas and what kinds of brushes he used to achieve the great detail in the bird's wing feathers. He politely answered all the questions. Then someone asked him how long it took to complete the painting. A big smile spread across his wrinkled face.

"A lifetime," he replied.

He went on to explain how, as a boy, he had hiked the woods of central Wisconsin, become acquainted with the out-of-doors, and absorbed information about fall colors and the behavior of ruffed grouse, Canada geese, mallard ducks, and a host of other wildlife native to the area.

His audience looked a bit perplexed. Finally, he said, "An artist has to have many skills. I must know how to mix paint to achieve subtle colors. I must know which brush to use when and how to hold it and how to apply paint to it. But what is most important for me as a painter, what makes my work art, I can't explain to you. I know how to do it. I couldn't begin to tell you what it is. I suspect this 'knowledge,' if it is knowledge, is something that is deep within me, something that draws on skills I've learned but goes a great distance beyond skills."

So it is for leadership. Certain basic competencies such as communication and interpersonal relationships continue to be important. Skills beyond these will emerge as leaders invent them by participating in new situations. Beyond skills, adult education leaders require that difficult-to-describe "something extra" that separates an everyday painter from an artist.

Developing Leadership Capacity

The new perspective on adult education leadership focuses on developing leadership capacity. The dimensions of leadership capacity include (1) the ability to reflect while acting and then make appropriate adjustments (specific leadership contexts often require unique leadership approaches), (2) acquiring leadership competencies that apply to many leadership contexts, and (3) evolving a personal philosophy of leadership.

Adult education leaders in the emerging age must develop the capacity for acting and reflecting and for designing and redesigning action as they perform it. These leaders practice what Donald Schön (1983) describes as reflection in action. They make adjustments in what they are doing while they are doing it. Drawing on Schön's work, I would describe the process roughly as follows:

1. We enter a leadership situation and are surprised with what we find—it may be pleasant or unpleasant, but what we find doesn't fit what we had expected.

2. We immediately ask, "What am I experiencing? What have I come upon?" We try to perceive the situation as accurately as we can, looking for examples in our supply of approaches that we might try, but not being too upset if we come up with nothing. We try to learn as much about the situation as possible, trying to avoid allowing panic to take over when we conclude that we haven't experienced anything quite like this before. Realizing that our past experience and our beliefs and values influence what we experience, we try to examine the situation from every possible perspective. We "bracket" our own biases as much as possible so that we are able to perceive as complete a picture of the situation as we possibly can.

3. We try something and immediately reflect on what we did. We continue doing what seems to work and stop doing what doesn't. As we experiment, we constantly reflect on what works and what doesn't. We see mistakes as merely steps toward learning rather than as failure. For many leaders, this approach to leadership requires a transformation in thinking.

Most of us have been trained to believe that out there somewhere is a theory, a how-to article or book, or a guide sheet that gives directions for most, if not all, leadership situations. The reality is that many situations today bear little or no resemblance to yesterday's leadership situations. Leaders increasingly come up with leadership approaches on the spot—to what extent depends on the context. In some volatile and rapidly changing contexts, a majority of leadership approaches may not be known to the leader prior to acting on them.

In less volatile situations, traditional leadership approaches continue to be effective. One task for today's leaders is assessing the nature of the leadership context in which they find themselves. Sometimes the leader does not know what to do. The key is to start doing and then reflect on the results and fine-tune as the situation plays out.

An administrator leader—I'll call him Joseph—in a western state is given the assignment of improving relations between an Indian reservation and the community adjacent to it. The area has a long history of animosity between the two groups, characterized by much distrust and frequent name-calling. Joseph, himself a Native American, is generally respected by members of the tribe living on the reservation. He began by setting up a series of meetings between representatives of the tribe and representatives of the community. There was no agenda at these early meetings, no attempts at formal situational analysis, no blueprint for action. Representatives of both sides simply talked and talked. They worked slowly to understand each other as human beings, with many common interests, even though their backgrounds were so different.

From time to time I talked with Joseph about the group's activities. Sometimes he was despondent. "Jerry, this thing is just not working. Sometimes I believe these two groups don't want to understand each other." At other times he was more optimistic. "We just added three more people to our group, and I finally think we accomplished something at our last meeting."

These meetings have been going on for more than two years. Joseph believes that one of the important outcomes of the effort is that the two groups continue to talk. He is extremely patient and believes that with a solid base of understanding, this diverse group will accomplish much.

When I spoke with him about the leadership approaches he was using, he hesitated. "You know, Jerry," he replied. "There isn't a whole lot that I learned about leadership that works here. Sure, I know about being patient, and I know how to listen. But mostly I make it up as I go. And frankly, I don't know what to expect each time I meet with this group. I just pay attention to what is going on and do my best."

Fundamental to building leadership capacity are a positive attitude and well-developed skills for continuous learning. With leaders constantly buffeted by stormy-weather change, learning is one of the few constants in a leader's life. Leaders learn their way through situations where the challenges are enormous and where most rules and recipes of the past no longer apply. The greatest capacity that any leader can develop is the capacity to learn and then immediately apply those lessons. Learning and acting on the learning are practically simultaneous, different from the past, when we had the luxury of learning and reflecting and then at some later time applying the results.

Beyond having the ability and the confidence to make it up as they go, certain leadership competencies, including the following, apply in many leadership situations:

Communication skills: the ability to write clearly, speak concisely, and listen accurately

Human relations skills: the ability to relate well to people, including the art of negotiation

Well-developed thinking skills: the ability to think creatively as well as think critically

Perception skills: the ability to see the big picture and the relationship of the parts to the whole

A sense of time: the ability to see the relationship of the past to the present with an eye toward the future

Question-framing skills: the ability to examine situations and frame questions that encourage deeper examination and analysis

Reflection skills: the ability to reflect and learn from the reflection

Abstraction skills: the ability to make meaning from ambiguous and sometimes chaotic situations

Learning skills: the ability to assimilate new material and methods and then act on them

Having a personal leadership philosophy is a fundamental capacity for leaders in the emerging age. When the world seems to be falling down around us, knowing what we believe and value in the midst of chaos and confusion can help keep us settled and focused. Developing a personal philosophy of leadership is the topic of the next chapter.

Chapter Four

Developing a Personal Philosophy of Leadership

With leadership contexts constantly changing and with leaders needing to lead in different ways in response to these changing conditions, many look for a beacon to help them find their way. A personal philosophy of leadership can be such a beacon.

Without a leadership philosophy, contexts can pull leaders this way and that, sometimes to the point that a leader does not know what to do. Early in my career I was responsible for adult education programs in horticulture in an urban community. The context at first appeared straightforward and uncontentious. But soon two opposing groups made sure that I knew their perspectives. One group came out strongly for using chemicals to control garden pests, arguing that chemicals were safe, efficient, and economical. The second group, consisting of organic gardeners and representatives of various environmental groups, shunned chemical pesticides, advocating instead natural approaches to pest control.

I must confess that in those days, I had not thought much about my philosophy of leadership. But issues like chemical pesticide use got my attention and forced me to think clearly about what I believed and valued and, in the midst of this seemingly impossible quandary, how I could provide educational leadership.

My supervisor told me to quit worrying about the organic gardeners and environmentalists because I had good scientific research to back my chemical recommendations. And once the organic gardeners learned about the advantages of chemical pest control, they would start using chemicals, he believed.

The organic gardeners reminded me that they paid taxes, too, and were entitled to my assistance. After considerable thought, I decided to work with both groups, valuing the diversity of perspectives and believing that these two groups might have some positive influence on each other. I even arranged an educational program where gardeners representing each perspective had their say. I also believed that it was important for each group to understand my position, even though neither group agreed with it. My supervisor, to his credit, simply said, "We'll wait and see what happens."

This all happened many years ago (the issues still remain). For me, at that time, figuring out what I believed and valued helped me make sense out of the situation and continue to provide educational leadership, more authentically and ethically, I believe, than if I had chosen only to work with the gardeners who wanted up-to-date information about chemical pesticides.

Today's adult education contexts are no different. Having a personal philosophy of leadership can provide needed direction for often harried leaders, no matter what their leadership position in an organization. A large continuing education organization in a western state was undergoing a reorganization and a redirection of its adult education programs. The director attended workshops on developing a personal philosophy of leadership. A year or so later, I talked with him about the values of a leadership philosophy and how he had applied his philosophy to the challenges he faced in an organization that was undergoing profound change. He told me that developing a personal philosophy of leadership had been one of the most important things he had recently done. "I am continually updating it," he said. "And not a day goes by that I don't relate something I'm doing, some decision I'm making, to my philosophy. It's not that I didn't have a leadership philosophy before— I think I did. But by spending time systematically exploring my basic beliefs and values, my leadership philosophy has gained much more depth." He went on to tell me that he is encouraging all of his middle managers to put their personal leadership philosophies in writing. "It helps administrators to think and put into focus what is important in their lives, and what is important for the organization," he said. "Leadership philosophy is particularly important on days when little seems to make sense in my job."

A personal philosophy of leadership, which includes major components of a philosophy for living, can be a beacon for surviving and even looking forward to the stormy weather of many adult education leadership positions. A well-thought-out personal philosophy of leadership becomes a center for one's life, a touchstone that can be returned to again and again.

Components of a Philosophy of Leadership

I use the diagram of a flower to explain an approach for developing a personal philosophy of leadership (see Figure 4.1). For me, adult education leadership consists of leaders, what they do, what results from what they do, and the educational setting in which they work. Thus each petal of the flower represents one aspect of leadership: leader qualities and characteristics, leadership approaches, expected leadership outcomes, and educational perspectives. In reflecting on what information to include for each petal, leaders carefully examine their own beliefs about these components and the contexts in which they work. For instance, leadership approaches that work well in cooperative extension may not work as well in an adult literacy organization, a museum, or a library. Likewise, leadership approaches used in a major firm's executive development program will likely differ from a community college's continuing education program.

At one time I was an army officer responsible for a railroad transportation company. The army's leadership manual was very clear about what I should do, how I should do it, and what to do if someone did not follow my orders. Years later, I became a departmental chair at a university. There was no leadership manual;

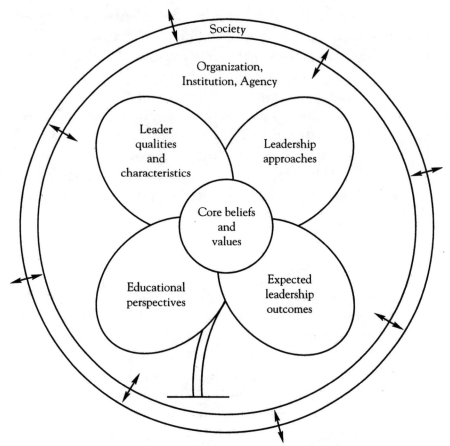

Figure 4.1. A Philosophy for Leadership.

indeed, there were few guidelines of any sort. In our department the chair did not give orders. An entirely different set of leadership approaches was required, including sharing responsibility, developing team approaches to problems, making connections with groups outside the department, and keeping departmental members informed on matters that affected them. This comparison is not to suggest that the army approach to leading was somehow lacking. The military is quite a different context from a university department and requires quite different leadership approaches.

The core of a leadership philosophy includes the leader's fundamental beliefs and values about reality, people, knowledge, ethics, and aesthetics. Also, a leadership philosophy is always developed in context. This context includes the leader's organization, the local and larger community, and even a global context. As argued in Chapter Two, the emerging age, with its challenges, is one dimension of the broader context that must be reckoned with when developing a leadership philosophy.

Importance of a Personal Philosophy of Leadership

Often in my leadership workshops, when I emphasize writing personal philosophy statements some participants will say, "I know what I believe and what I value. Why should I take time to write this down?" There are several reasons.

The process of writing down our beliefs and values causes us to examine them as we write. In the process of writing we ask ourselves, "Do I really believe this? Is this really a value of mine?" By writing down our beliefs and values, we refine them from partially developed and incomplete thoughts into more definite thoughts. Even if we do not show our philosophy statement to anyone else, the process of writing it makes it seem more public. The writing process moves thinking from mind to paper. For some people this move is an immense leap.

The process of writing can be a clarifying process. When we begin to write, we may not be clear about our thoughts, but as we write, for many of us the fog lifts and clarity emerges. Also, as we write, we may discover huge gaps between what we thought we knew and what we actually know. Writing brings these gaps into focus. The opposite is also true. As we write, we discover things that we knew but were not aware that we knew. For many people, the process of writing is a way of getting in touch with the unconscious, the place in our mind where vast quantities of thoughts, ideas, feelings, facts, and perspectives are stored and, we think, forgotten.

The process of writing a personal philosophy statement is a way of putting our beliefs and values in priority order. We often do this unknowingly. But the items that appear on the top of our list are often what we prize most highly and feel most strongly about. Although our personal philosophy of leadership can serve as a touchstone for decision making, acting, reacting, and confronting stormy weather, it too is subject to change and modification. Having our personal philosophy in writing provides a checkpoint as we wrestle with and make changes in some of our beliefs and values. Also, for those who are working at clarifying and perhaps deepening their personal philosophies of leadership, a written statement is one that can be shared with a friend or colleague and serve as a basis for discussion.

Guide for Writing a Personal Leadership Philosophy

Following is a guide for writing a personal philosophy of leadership:

1. Write a Summary Statement of Your Leadership Context

There are contextual dimensions to the emerging age I described in Chapter Two that impinge on all organizations and their leaders. But in addition to responding to the contextual demands of the emerging age, leaders must be well aware of other contextual dimensions.

Successful leaders learn all they can about their organization's structure, politics, history, values, beliefs, and environment. Henry Mintzberg (1973) says the leader's work is influenced by four dimensions of context: (a) the organization and its milieu; (b) the job itself, its level within the organization, and the function for which it has responsibility—overall organizational leadership, programming, budgeting, personnel, and so on; (c) the person in the job—effects of personality and style; and (d) situational variables such as seasonal variations or temporary budget threats. These four factors interact to create a constantly changing context for the leader.

Context is complicated and often contradictory. For instance, it is essential that adult education leaders know the culture of their organization well. Leaders must also know the community that their organization serves, its expectations, the history of relationships between the local community and the organization, and other relevant facts.

Often in the study of these multiple contexts, the leader will uncover contradictions. The emerging age may provide a set of assumptions and an approach to thinking quite different from the assumptions held by some organizations. On which context should a leader focus attention? As paradoxical as it sounds, the answer is all of them. Acting in the unchanging, traditional context that characterizes some adult education organizations will frustrate leaders who know and accept many of the assumptions of the emerging age. Yet leaders know that they must attend to the context that pays their salaries and at the same time challenge the context to move forward. Patience and understanding are key strategies.

Recently I learned about a university president who was a great supporter of continuing education and an innovator in organizational renewal and creative ways of providing educational opportunities. This president's motto was "The train is leaving; either get on or get out of the way." Some people viewed him as wanting to move too fast, and he was asked to resign. He misread the context in which he was working.

To begin describing the context for your organization, start with a copy of your organization's mission statement. Include a statement about your organization's beliefs and values, if this is available. Many organizations are making such statements explicit and putting them in writing. If your organization does not have such a statement, write a few statements about what you think your organization believes and values.

As part of the context statement, include information about the people your organization serves—who they are, what they expect from you, what you expect from them, and so on. Some of this information may be part of your organization's mission statement. Comment also about people you believe your organization should serve and currently serves inadequately or not at all.

What societal changes are now affecting your organization or are likely to in the near future? Some of these changes may be global in nature, others more local. Some may be immediate, others more distant.

Include statements about your own place in the organization—where you fit and what you are expected to do. What is your job description? Include a capsule summary of your career in the organization, the positions you have held, what you believe you have accomplished, and what major hurdles you have faced.

How does your organization view leaders, leadership approaches, outcomes of leadership, and educational perspectives? These of course vary from context to context.

• _Leader qualities and characteristics_. (See Chapter Six.) How would you describe the current leaders in your organization? What qualities do they have that you believe are consistent with the challenges of the emerging age? In what ways are they contradictory? Are there individuals who believe they must be in control at all times? Are there individuals who rely on the past as a predictor of the future?

What qualities and characteristics do employees in your organization want in their leaders? Do they expect take-charge individuals in administrative leadership positions? Do they expect their leaders to be solely committed to the organization, with little time for anything else? What skills do they expect their leaders to have?

How do you describe yourself as a leader? How do the leader characteristics and qualities you possess match up with those (to be described in Chapter Six) such as passion, courage, skill building, feeling comfortable with paradox, the ability to reflect on actions, and skill in seeing the big picture and multiple relationships?

How do your leader qualities and characteristics compare with the requirements of the emerging age and the demands of the context in which you work?

• *Outcomes for leadership.* (See Chapter Seven.) What does your organization believe its leaders ought to accomplish? Does it expect them to provide direction for developing a vision and mission statements and then see to it that the various plans are carried out? Does it expect leaders to provide a work environment where employees can express their potential? What value does the organization place on outcomes that go beyond the mission statement and regard for employees, such as concern for diversity, quality, social awareness, collaboration, and collective spirituality?

What do you believe ought be the outcomes of leadership efforts? How do your beliefs compare with your organization's beliefs about outcomes for leadership efforts? How do your beliefs about leadership outcomes square with the leadership outcomes required of the emerging age?

• *Leadership approaches.* (See Chapter Eight.) How do the leaders in your organization lead? What strategies do they follow? How do they make decisions? Do they involve or exclude people? In what ways? Do they subscribe to competitive or collaborative leadership approaches? How do they handle power? Do they share power? If so, how? Do they follow approaches that you believe will be required of adult education leaders in the emerging age?

How do you believe your organization wants its leaders to act? Is the situation a dependent one, where employees are constantly looking to leaders for answers and direction? To what extent are employees asking for more involvement in the organization's leadership functions?

What leadership approaches do you use? How do the leadership approaches you use compare with the approaches required for the emerging age, such as sharing power, inspiring, renewing, teaching, vision making, challenging, using humor, building bridges, tolerating and sometimes encouraging discomfort, and encouraging artistry?

- *Educational perspectives*. (See Chapter Nine.) How does your organization view teachers and teaching, learners and learning, and the future direction for education? Is educational technology an important consideration in your organization? How would you describe the students who participate in the various programs? How would you describe the teaching processes used in the organization? How do participants react to the teaching? How is educational quality defined in the organization? To what extent is educational quality defined by the learners? To what extent do participants believe that what they are learning is relevant, challenging, and consistent with their reasons for participating?

What are your beliefs about the process of education? Are they consistent with the beliefs of your organization? How do they jibe with the challenges of the emerging age?

2. Write a Statement of Your Fundamental Beliefs and Values

The core of a personal philosophy of leadership includes statements about your fundamental beliefs and values. As Stephen Covey (1989) argues, "People can't live with change if there's not a changeless core inside them. The key to the ability to change is a changeless sense of who you are, what you are about and what you value" (p. 108).

The nature of self, with the associated fundamental beliefs and values, is the core of our being; it defines who we are and guides what we do and how we do it. Thus, understanding our core beliefs and values is fundamental. Let us now turn to a discussion of fundamental beliefs and values, which begins with a discussion of the self.

Components of Self. The self has three components—the mind, the body, and the spirit. As Srivastva, Cooperrider, and Associates (1990) point out, "Everyone is talking about paradigm shifts and moving from the Industrial Age to the Information Age, but few are talking about the qualities of the mind, body, and spirit that are involved in executing such shifts, to say nothing of leading others in making the shift" (p. 332).

In my judgment, it is essential that leaders for the new perspective on adult education leadership be well acquainted with mind, body, and spirit and the relationships among them. As Figure 4.2 suggests, there is a close relationship among these three components, so close that problems often result when one of the three is ignored or is not functioning well. If we are ill, our mind doesn't function well and our spirit languishes. If we concentrate excessively on body building but do nothing to enhance our spiritual and mental dimensions, we become shallow. If we concentrate on mental development but overlook spirit and body, we may put our physical and mental health in jeopardy.

Not only are spirit, mind, and body closely related, but the self also relates to a larger context. None of us lives in isolation; we are influenced by our context and we in turn influence it. We are all part of a community that ranges from one other person to many people. The context for the self includes how we relate to others, individually and collectively. It encompasses our relationship with the natural world and, for many people, a spiritual relationship outside the self. Our beliefs about self also relate to how we think

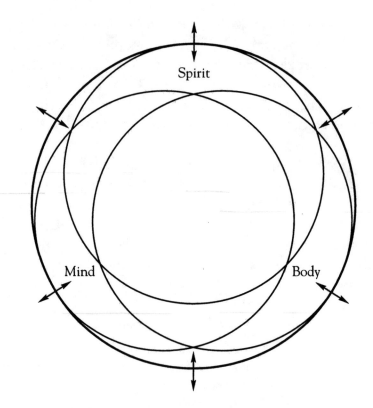

Figure 4.2 Nature of Self.

about leader qualities and characteristics, about leadership approaches, expected leadership outcomes, and educational perspectives.

Beyond the immediate relationships, the self is also dramatically influenced by personal history. As discussed in Chapter Ten, who we are (our self) contains beliefs and values that trace back to our earliest beginnings. We are not aware of many of these beliefs and values, yet all, known and unknown, influence who we are and how we behave. In Chapter Five I discuss conscious and unconscious beliefs and values and how they influence who we are, what we do, and often even what we perceive. Most of us have a store of unconscious beliefs and values hidden deep within us, yet they often have more influence on us than the beliefs and values of which we are aware.

Mind, Body, and Spirit: Some Descriptions. Our mind has the ability to think and to feel, the capacity to be rational and logical, and the potential to be creative and intuitive. Some experts suggest that the mind has two sides, a right side that favors intuition, sensing, and feeling, and a left side that is more logical, organized, judgmental, and numerical. The right side of the brain is more visual and concerned with seeing "big pictures"; it is more concerned with patterns than with details. The right side of the brain is involved with bringing things together and seeing relationships among pieces. The left side of the brain, according to researchers, is systematic, objective, rational, and interested in detail.

Our bodies are born, they age, and they die, in a somewhat predictable manner. They have survival and sexual needs. They require regular exercise or they become dysfunctional. They are susceptible to disease and illness. We believe we have control over some aspects of our bodies; many aspects, however, operate beyond our control or even our awareness. Much is known about our bodies as researchers continue to poke and probe, test and experiment. But a great deal about our bodies remains mysterious, unknown. Our bodies are the unpredictable, wonderful, painful, joyful, and disappointing containers of our lives. Many of us treat them as if they were mechanical constructions that will last forever. Some of us assume that all that is required is a little repair work from time to time, a yearly checkup like we give our automobiles, and our body will function with little or no attention.

The spirit is another matter. Many of us deny that there is such a thing as the spirit. Some argue that we already give too much importance to feelings when we talk about the mind and that adding a discussion of spirit really goes too far. Some argue, forcefully, that spirit is an artifact of a primitive being, someone who depended on the unseen and the unknown to give solace and direction to life. Thanks to research and science, these persons argue, the matter of spirit can be buried and properly forgotten. Others take quite a different position. For instance, Srivastva, Cooperrider, and Associates (1990) write, "Leaders tend not to be satisfied with being merely technically correct. They want to be correct consistent with their deeper beliefs about what is important and about what the meaning of their life is. . . . In this sense, then, *spiritual condition* refers to the degree to which the person acts on values that transcend the sheer material conditions and events of the world, that is, on values that are not contingent for their validity on these conditions and events" (p. 334).

Peter Vaill (1989) says that spirituality is "to pay more attention to one's own spiritual qualities, feelings, insights, and yearnings. It is to reach more deeply into oneself for that which is unquestionably authentic. It is to attune oneself to those truths one considers timeless and unassailable, the deepest principles one knows" (p. 31).

Spirit is very private and deep within us. Many people argue that spirit is the most fundamental dimension of our being, the one that makes us human. It is our spirit that helps get us up each morning and supports us through the day. Our language recognizes the value of the spirit in our lives. We say, "You're in good spirits today" or "They had a spirited discussion."

Many people's spiritual side has been buried by years of misuse and neglect. It remains a submerged, perhaps wounded entity crying to be recognized, released, and nourished. One's spirit is refreshed and enhanced in many ways. For some people, organized religion enhances the spirit. They pray, meditate, and participate in religious celebrations and rituals and feel stimulated, refreshed, and reassured.

Others renew their spirit through music and dance and through literature and drama. Still others find their spirits enhanced by participating in creative activities. They write, make art or music, or perform on the stage. Some renew their spirit by returning again and again to nature, to hearing the primitive call of the loon and the sound of a canoe paddle dipping into the blue waters of an isolated lake. And, of course, many people combine these spirit renewing activities.

Identifying Fundamental Beliefs and Values. To begin understanding who we are, it is helpful to identify and then examine our fundamental beliefs and values. These beliefs and values guide and influence what we do and how we do it. Even more fundamentally, our beliefs and values influence how we think and even how we perceive the world around us and what we notice in it. For instance, a leader's beliefs about human nature have an important influence on how this person leads. If a leader believes that people are largely motivated externally, through salary, rewards, and recognition, the leader will lead differently than one who believes that people are largely internally motivated and want more control over themselves and their workplace. (Chapter Five provides more information about beliefs and values and how to analyze them.)

House as a Metaphor for Personal Beliefs and Values. One way to begin examining fundamental beliefs and values is to consider our personal belief-and-value system as a house. Our fundamental values are the foundation, walls, beams, and posts—all the elements that keep our house erect and sturdy.

Assume that our house has three major rooms, with doors and hallways connecting them. One room is the "reality-people room," one the "knowledge" room, and one the "ethics-aesthetics" room. Each room has furniture in it. Let's refer to this furniture as our beliefs. The furniture is for the most part unique to the room in which it is found. One generally finds kitchen furniture in the kitchen, bedroom furniture in the bedroom, and so on. Likewise, in our knowledge room we'll expect to find what we believe about knowledge, the sources of knowledge, and how we come to know things. In the reality-people room we'll look for beliefs about the nature of human beings, of time, and of organizations and how they work. And in the ethics-aesthetics room we'll find beliefs about what is right and wrong, good and bad, beautiful and ugly, attractive and repellant.

In each room the beliefs are ours. This is our house. At the moment, we aren't interested in what furniture ought to be in the various rooms or has at one time been there. For this exercise, we are interested in how these rooms are currently furnished with beliefs and values.

As we begin to examine the furniture in our house, we find furnishings (beliefs) that clash. We may have an antique chair and a modern chair in the same room, and they may be crowding each other, competing for the same space. Or we may find modern furniture in the kitchen and worn-out, hardly serviceable furniture in the living room, which is to say that we may have examined our beliefs about knowledge but have done little over the years examining beliefs about human beings and their motivations, interests, and basic nature.

Here are some specific questions to help identify the furniture in each of the rooms in your house.

- *Reality.* What do you believe about the nature of time? Are we moving forward in an incremental, linear fashion, or is time more cyclical, like seasonal change or day and night? Is there such a thing as progress? Is reality something that is fixed, on which several people can agree? Or are there multiple realities, each in the eye of the beholder? In other words, can I say that I have a right to my reality and you have a right to yours? Is a person's reality ever wrong? Is it possible for someone's reality to be more right than someone else's? By what criteria can we judge the "rightness" of someone's reality? Is it proper to do such judging? What is the difference between illusion and reality?

- *People.* What do you believe about human nature? About the relationship of people to the natural world? About the relationship of people to each other? What do you believe motivates people to action? What do you believe prevents people from taking charge of their lives? To what extent do you believe that culture, socioeconomic status, race, and gender influence how people perceive, learn, react, and are motivated? How does your spiritual self define who you are? How does your spiritual self relate to your actions?

- *Knowledge.* What is knowledge? Is it created, discovered, or both? What is the relationship of knowledge to facts, ideas, opinions, perspectives? By what means do we come to know something? How do we affirm the validity of our knowledge? What is the source of our knowing—empirical evidence? Intuition emerging from our unconscious? Experts who claim special knowledge? Our own rational thought processes? Some combination of these? To what extent are we unaware of what we know? To what extent does this unknown knowledge unconsciously guide our thoughts, feelings, and actions? Can we become aware of our buried knowledge?

What do we believe about the relationship of perception to knowing? How do our personal histories influence how we come to know things? What is the relationship of research to knowledge? How do research paradigms influence the results of research? That is, might we expect different outcomes from a traditional positivistic research approach and a naturalistic research approach?

Is there such a thing as wisdom? If so, who has it? Is there such a thing as truth? If truth exists, are there universal truths or only individual truths? Can each of us have our own truth? Should each of us strive to have our own truth? How does truth relate to knowledge? Can we have knowledge and not have truth? How does having truth relate to taking charge of our lives?

- *Aesthetics.* What are our beliefs about aesthetics? Is aesthetics more than paintings, artistic creations, and such? Can we have aesthetics in our lives that includes the arts but is not limited to them? What does it mean to lead aesthetically? Can that actually be done? How do we differentiate an environment that is aesthetic from one that is not?

- *Ethics.* How do we define ethics? Where do they fit in our lives and in our leadership? How do we practice ethical leadership? How do we judge what is ethical and what is not? Do we believe that all ethical decisions are situational? If not, how do we decide a universal ethic from one that appears to be situational? What do we believe about ethical decision making?

Examples of fundamental values to consider are honesty, concern for family, commitment to children, integrity, being a citizen of the globe, justice, human rights, fairness, concern for nature and the physical environment, and faith in a spiritual being. Each of us has a different set of values, but many of us have common values as well. (See Chapter Five for a further description of values and their interrelationships.)

3. Write a Personal Credo Statement

Writing a personal credo is one way to begin uncovering basic values and beliefs about ourselves. Most of us have a personal credo that guides us like a map guides a traveler. Unfortunately for some of us, our personal credo is buried. We have not taken time to reflect on what we fundamentally believe and value, and hence we allow expediency, pragmatism, politics, exhaustion, boredom, group-think (because others do it this way, so must I), and a host of other factors to influence what we do and ultimately who we are.

Without a personal credo, we are like a hiker without a compass, following this trail and that, never quite sure where we are going but exceedingly busy nonetheless. Without a compass, the hiker, encountering divergent paths, has no basis for deciding which path to take. The compassless hiker is susceptible to all kinds of often contradictory advice about which trail to take: take the north trail; you'll get there faster. Take the south trail; the view is better. Soon the hiker knows not what trail to take, if any. Some hikers, confronting divergent trails, turn around and hike on yesterday's path, comforted by the familiar surroundings. They have returned to their past. Other hikers become exceedingly uncomfortable with the multiple opportunities, so they set up a permanent base camp, fearful that no trail is the "right" trail. They become paralyzed in the present.

Of course, it is not difficult to see the relationship of the compassless hiker to the compassless adult education leader: both are stymied by contradictory advice, stick with familiar ways of doing things, are uncomfortable with multiple opportunities, and yet are exceedingly busy. A personal credo becomes a foundation for action, a bright beacon in a foggy night. The administrative "hiker," with credo in hand, moves with confidence in an ever more confusing, changing, and challenging world. A personal credo also becomes the core for a working philosophy of leadership.

All of this is not to say that one's credo becomes a fixed entity, set for life. On the contrary, parts of one's credo come repeatedly under review. Just as a hiker at various times is likely to check if the compass is working properly, so must we all from time to time examine our credos. Credos, like everything else in a changing world, can become out-of-date.

A personal credo is a statement that reflects fundamental beliefs and values but also shows direction. Beliefs and values are statements of *who you are* as a human being. A credo statement expresses *what you want to be* and *what you want to do* based on who you are. A credo statement becomes your personal guide, a lighthouse in stormy weather, a compass when the fog is so thick you don't know which way to turn. Credo statements are the least likely to change of anything about you. As Stephen Covey (1989, p. 107) says, they are our personal constitutions.

What sorts of things does one write in a credo statement? Credos are unique to the person writing them. There is neither a single acceptable style nor a standard set of statements. Below are examples of credo statements written by participants in various workshops I have conducted. (This list is illustrative but is in no way intended to be all-inclusive.)

I will balance work time with family and personal time.

I will work hard but will not make excuses for taking vacations and days off to relax.

Solitude and personal reflection are important parts of my life. I will seek them daily.

If I can't do something well, I will not accept the task. I also recognize that a fetish for perfection can sometimes paralyze action.

I will be open to new ideas and perspectives, recognizing how difficult that can be at times.

I will work harder to be open to people of diverse backgrounds and perspectives, realizing that great and wonderful things can result when people of diversity learn to pool the wonders of their differences to create something more than the sum of what and who they are.

I will constantly remind myself, when confronted with a new situation, that how I read the situation is largely influenced by who I am and where I have been in my life.

New ideas are important to me, from a wide array of sources, from the sciences and arts, from the humanities and the person on the street. I must learn to receive new ideas with all my senses, not merely my eyes and ears.

I will regularly write my reflections on the meaning of what I am doing and why I am doing it.

Regularly, I will create something new—a new idea, a new relationship, a new structure.

I recognize the power of a being that is outside me but is tied to my spiritual self.

My spiritual self, although often mysterious and inaccessible, is a most important dimension of my humanness and my fundamental being. It helps me be more of a *human being* rather than merely a *human doing.*

My body is the only one I have; I must cherish it and care for it. I must learn to hear and heed its signals to slow down, to exercise more, to attend more carefully to what I eat.

I will encourage my children to be what they want to be, not what I want them to be.

I will celebrate each day as a gift and respond to that gift by giving of myself to my work, my family, and others freely and openly.

I will learn one new thing each day.

I will recognize that I can choose to be angry or happy and work at choosing the latter.

I am committed to my own personal growth—intellectually, physically, emotionally, and spiritually.

I will take time to reflect on the good things in life every day. I will identify at least three good things that happened each day.

I will focus as much creative energy on myself and my well-being as I do on my work.

I will be patient and listen to my family. I will give them the same support and respect as I give to my professional colleagues and clients.

I will expect nothing from others beyond what I myself would do.

In writing credo statements, avoid such expressions as "I will try," "I will work toward," and other tentative language that falls short of complete commitment. There is a considerable difference between saying you *will try to* do something and saying you *will* do something.

Conclusion

To summarize, a philosophy of leadership includes (1) a summary statement of the leader's context, (2) a statement of the leader's fundamental beliefs and values, and (3) the leader's personal credo statement.

In my experience, leaders learn a great deal about themselves through the process of writing their philosophies of leadership. But the work is never done. Smart leaders who have written their philosophies revisit them from time to time, changing, revising, and developing more in-depth statements about their beliefs, values, and credo statements. Knowledge of one's beliefs and values provides a foundation for action in an increasingly chaotic world where organizations are changing constantly and the leader's role is always evolving. Having a well-thought-out personal philosophy of leadership is the essence of the new leadership perspective on adult education. The emerging age requires that people be well grounded in what they believe and value but at the same time know intimately the context in which they work.

Chapter Five

Examining Beliefs and Values About Leadership

As I argued in Chapter Four, a foundation for adult education leadership for the emerging age is for leaders to develop a personal philosophy of leadership. The core of a leadership philosophy consists of a leader's personal beliefs and values. In this chapter I explore how to identify and begin analyzing beliefs and values.

A *belief* is what we accept as truth. Daryl Bem (1970) says a belief is a perception of "some relationship between two things or between some thing and a characteristic of it" (p. 4). *Values* are principles that guide and give organizations and individuals a sense of direction, criteria for worth, and a sense of moral and ethical foundation. Bem defines a value as "a primitive preference for or a positive attitude toward certain end-states of existence (like equality, salvation, self-fulfillment, or freedom), or certain broad modes of conduct (like courage, honesty, friendship, or chastity)" (p. 16).

Conflicting Beliefs and Values

Individual and organizational beliefs and values often interact and may conflict. When I worked as a youth leader for an adult education organization, my primary responsibility was recruiting and training volunteer leaders. Most of the youth and volunteer leaders involved in the program were from white, middle-class families in the area. One day I suggested to my supervisor that I wanted to do some recruiting and training on a nearby Indian reservation. I had made some initial contacts with the tribal leaders and knew of their interest.

My supervisor said, "I'm not sure this is a good idea. You realize that your first responsibility is to the leaders you already work with."

I replied that I would like to try it anyway. A large number of young people lived on the reservation, and I believed they would find our programs interesting and useful.

"When the program we hired you to do is without flaw, then you can work with the Indians," my supervisor said.

Here was a clear case where two sets of beliefs came into conflict, an individual's (mine) and the organization's (my supervisor's). I did work on the Indian reservation, and I did keep my job, but the value differences between me and my organization on this issue persisted.

Conflict between an adult education leader's beliefs and values and those of the larger community is almost inevitable. For example, an administrative leader believes that job training programs are the key to solving the problems of the poor in a core urban area. Certain community groups strongly disagree. They argue that until poor people gain political control over what affects them, education will not make much difference. Political control should come first; education may follow later. The adult education leader is left with the challenge of continuing with the educational program as organized or perhaps rethinking the educational program so that it would help citizens gain more political control in their community.

Contextual and Fundamental Beliefs and Values

Beliefs and values exist in layers (Sperry, 1981). The most fundamental beliefs and values undergird those that are less fundamental—what we could call contextual beliefs and values—and include beliefs and values about teaching and what it is; learning and how it occurs; knowledge and how it is discovered, created, and organized; learners and their characteristics; administrative leaders and how they perform; and educational institutions and their purposes (see Chapter Four). Other contextual beliefs and values include what we believe and value about human beings and the purposes of human life, competition and cooperation, the nature of time, progress, the individual and society, and the roles, relationships, and purposes of society's institutions.

Fundamental beliefs and values also include a moral dimension. From the 1960s to 1980s, much attention was given to value clarification, a process designed to help individuals and groups reveal and elucidate the values they held. For the facilitators of these groups, it didn't matter what values group members held as long as they were aware of them.

Today many people believe that unless certain values are promoted, life as we know it will cease to exist. For example, William Bennett (1993), a former U.S. secretary of education, has written a best-selling book that specifies values that he believes are important for society (he calls them virtues). The values he discusses are self-discipline, compassion, responsibility, friendship, work, courage, perseverance, honesty, loyalty, and faith.

Other people are concerned about which fundamental values are of most importance for the continuation of life on this planet. Sperry (1981), for example, argues that certain values transcend time, space, culture, and geography, so important are they to the continuation of life. According to Sperry, "the most basic value of all, that which ought undergird all of our values and beliefs as our top social priority today, is to effect a change worldwide in [our] sense of value. This translates into hierarchic values theory as a change in what is held most sacred. What is needed, more specifically, is a new ethic, ideology, or theology that will make it sacrilegious to deplete natural resources, to pollute the environment, to overpopulate, to erase or degrade other species, or to otherwise destroy or defile the evolving quality of the biosphere" (p. 9). Sperry goes on to argue that unless environmental issues are given primary value, it doesn't matter in the long run what values are next in order.

What about the scantity of human life? What is the worth of a human being?

Other fundamental beliefs and values may include equal opportunity for people, honesty, justice, human rights (including the
rights to housing, health care, education, and freedom of speech),
and respect for diversity. Most adult education administrative leaders—and organizations, too—have wrestled with these values and
continue to do so. Generally, though, I believe that there is some
agreement that these bedrock beliefs and values ought to pervade
all that leaders and organizations do.

Conscious and Unconscious Beliefs and Values

Individuals and organizations are aware of some of the beliefs and
values that influence them. But they are also profoundly influenced
by beliefs and values of which they are not aware. These unconscious beliefs and values influence not only action but also perception. Thus unconscious beliefs and values can prevent people from
seeing things that may be obvious to others. We all wear blinders,
controlled often in large measure by our hidden beliefs and values.

Willis Harman (1988), Daryl Bem (1970), and Joseph Luft
(1969) all emphasize the importance and power of hidden beliefs
and values. Harman writes, "Each of us holds some set of beliefs
with which we conceptualize our experience—beliefs about history, beliefs about things, beliefs about the future, about what is
to be valued, or about what one ought to do. What may be less
obvious is that we have unconscious beliefs as well as conscious
ones" (p. 12).

Bem (1970) calls these hidden beliefs zero-order beliefs. He
says, "Our most fundamental primitive beliefs are so taken for
granted that we are apt not to notice that we hold them at all; we
remain unaware of them until they are called to our attention or
are brought into question by some bizarre circumstance in which
they appear to be violated" (p. 5). A basic characteristic of a zero-
order belief is not having an alternative to it. Sometimes, when we

become aware of alternative ways of thinking or acting, our unconscious zero-order beliefs flash into consciousness. Our initial immediate response is to oppose the alternative. Sometimes we are a bit surprised by our quick opposition. Part of the surprise is the uncovering of a belief that likely has been long buried in our unconscious memory.

Not long ago I worked with a large continuing education organization that was experiencing some problems. As we began examining the organization and how it operated, we together uncovered several beliefs about which several administrative leaders in the organization were not aware.

The organization's administrator sat at the top of organization's structure. Underneath her sat a row of associate administrators in the next layer of the organization chart, and still another layer of middle mangers under the associate administrators. I asked how all of this was working.

"We've got problems," someone offered, "both inside and outside the organization." Externally, communities and individuals requesting particular programs seldom received a response for six months or more. The organization had a system for reviewing such requests, and it required that they move though the tortuous layers of administrators as part of the decision-making process. In a few instances, by the time the organization was ready to respond, the problem had gone away, someone else had helped solve it, or it had transformed into quite a different problem.

Internally, the associate administrators, responsible for major program areas, had developed competitive relationships among themselves. They competed for funds, and they seldom shared information about what they were doing or with whom. As a result, many program needs that required the cooperation of programmers in more than one major unit were essentially ignored. Programmers who tried to work across program areas were penalized, particularly in terms of promotions and salary increases.

What hidden beliefs were uncovered?

1. *The way the organization is currently organized is appropriate and ought to continue.* We talked about alternatives to a hierarchal, top-down organization and the relative advantages and disadvantages of various structures given the demands of the emerging age.

2. *Competition among units within the organization is a strong motivator for greater productivity and innovation.* We discussed how competition within many organizations can be more negative than positive, particularly when it prevents interdisciplinary programming cooperation.

3. *The present system, in which programmers are evaluated within their respective units, has always worked well.* In reality, when programmers work cooperatively with programmers from other units, they are often penalized by their home units when promotions and merit increases are considered. When programmers are encouraged to do interdisciplinary work, they must be supported with innovative approaches for promotion and merit considerations, and so on. Uncovering their zero-order beliefs was the first step toward the organization's beginning to look at itself in depth and consider changes.

Individual Beliefs and Values

Individual beliefs and values fundamentally influence what leaders and followers do. These belief and value systems can stifle perception, smother innovation, and entrench the status quo. Or they can provide a solid foundation that supports and energizes the organization and its activities.

I recently talked with a dean who was attempting some new leadership arrangements within one of his departments. This department had major continuing education responsibilities, and the dean believed that the old system of having a single departmental head had not worked as well as it might. Rather than replace the department head, he suggested that the department take responsibility for creating a shared leadership approach. One person should have responsibility for undergraduate programs, another for graduate programs and research, another for continuing education, and so on. Five or six people in the department were to have responsibility for its administration and leadership. No one person was officially in charge.

A major challenge to this approach turned out to be the beliefs and values held by individuals within the department and by those who have contact with the department. When I asked the dean how this new approach was going, he said, "We continue to struggle, I think very productively, with the concept of shared leadership. But it is absolutely amazing how tied we are to the old hierarchical approach. The minute there is any tension, there is an immediate reversion to a top-down idea of structure. When there's a problem, people look for someone to come down with the answers. People have hidden within them the belief that this is the way organizations work, no matter what we do differently. There is a constant need to fight slipping into the one-person-in-charge approach."

Leaders for the emerging age are often challenged to make substantial changes in their organizations and how they work. But to do that, everyone involved must examine the fundamental beliefs and values they hold and how they will be affected by the changes.

Chris Argyris (1982) says that individuals and organizations that make slight adjustments in what they do but don't take time to examine their underlying beliefs and values are doing single-loop learning. "They are like a thermostat that corrects error (the room is too hot or too cold) without questioning its program (why am I set at 68 degrees?). If the thermostat did question its setting or why it should be measuring heat at all, that would require reex-

Becuz that's its job — to measure + regulate heat / temperature

amining the underlying program. This is called double-loop learning" (pp. xi–xii).

Organizations and individuals that do not examine their beliefs and values operate in a closed system. Day-to-day activities are influenced by the current set of beliefs and values, and in turn, the beliefs and values constantly reinforce organizational and individual action. This can go on indefinitely, as long as everything is going well. A comfortable circle of reinforcement can be challenged. A program fails. Participants roundly criticize what is done and how it is done, or they fail to show up at all. After several such failures or near failures, administrators began to wonder what is happening. They start fine-tuning (single-loop learning). Perhaps a more powerful instructor is needed, or perhaps more elaborate and up-to-date electronic media should be tried. The fine tuning is done, but the existing framework of beliefs and values is not examined.

The administrator begins to realize that the "standard approach" simply does not work, even when it is improved. This is of course the beginning of the transformation process (see Chapter Eleven), or what Thomas Kuhn (1970) calls a paradigm shift. Such a shift requires that the basic premises, the beliefs and values that guide action, be examined and perhaps dramatically changed.

A Process for Examining Beliefs and Values

A process for examining beliefs and values about leadership includes the following phases:

1. Identifying beliefs and values along various dimensions— reality, people, knowledge, aesthetics, and ethics
2. Searching for the roots of the uncovered beliefs and values
3. Becoming aware of feelings associated with beliefs and values
4. Attending to feelings

5. Comparing what leaders say they believe and value (espoused) with what they actually do (beliefs and values in action)

6. Comparing beliefs and values with the context in which leaders work and the requirements for leadership in the emerging age

7. Making judgments about beliefs and values in light of results from phases 5 and 6

This approach is a learning experience, but there are some interesting differences between examining beliefs and values and more traditional approaches to learning.

In more traditional approaches, we become aware of new ideas, new perspectives, and new ways of thinking, and then we compare these new things with what we already know, feel, believe, or understand. In the process of making comparisons between the new and what we already know, we discover that (1) the material is clearly new to us—there is nothing we now know to which we can make a comparison; (2) the new learning complements, expands, gives new meaning or perspective to what we already know; (3) the material contradicts or differs from what we already know or for some reason just doesn't feel right; or (4) some combination of these reactions.

Without examining the many reasons why we react to new learning in a particular way (previous learning, life experience, cultural influences, and so on), each response evokes different reactions and feelings.

For instance, we may be elated as we gain new knowledge, skills, and perspectives that we can quickly and easily add to our current repertoire. Or we may be angry, disappointed, frustrated, or uneasy confronting learning that somehow just doesn't fit. Baud and colleagues (1985) remind us that as we learn, we must attend to our feelings. "Depending on the circumstances and our intentions, we need either to work with our emotional responses, find ways of setting them aside, or if they are positive ones, retaining and enhancing them. If they do form barriers, these need to be recognized as such and removed before the learning process can proceed" (p. 29).

I would add a caution. Not only do we need to set aside some of our feelings and retain and enhance others, but we should also be leery of learning that seems to elicit only positive feelings. Such positive feelings may prevent us from critically examining both new learning and our own perspective for accepting it. Our cultural perspective and personal history are likely dictating our response. That is, we readily accept new learning with positive feelings if it appears to fit what we currently believe and value. Facing new learning that contradicts what we know often elicits negative feelings because it calls into question both the new learning and what we already know, believe, or value.

Let's return to examining beliefs and values as a learning experience. When examining beliefs and values, we start with what we believe, value, and feel about various aspects of leaders and leadership and then compare this knowledge with the contexts of our organization and the challenges of the emerging age.

Traditional learning could be described as an "outside-in" approach. Examining beliefs and values about leadership is an "inside-out" approach. We start where we are and spend some time examining the roots of our beliefs and values and our feelings about them. Then we look into the context of where we live and work and into the requirements of our leadership role to see whether our beliefs and values fit.

Contradictions Between Beliefs and Values Held and Actions Taken

Almost all of us, to a greater or lesser extent, say we believe and value something and then act as if we believe and value something else. An important part of examining beliefs and values about leadership is attending to the congruency between our words and our actions. A carefully developed set of beliefs and values that are neatly tucked into the far reaches of our minds but are not related to our day-to-day activity is hardly worth having. It is comparable to the business or educational institution that has a carefully developed mission statement but then ignores it and often contradicts what it says.

Contradictions between what we say we believe and value and how we act are not unusual. The important point is to recognize and come to grips with the contradictions. Several techniques can be used to spot such contradictions. Below I describe a pair of approaches for identifying beliefs and values. The first involves listing beliefs and values about leadership; the second, writing a story about a recently encountered situation.

Comparing the beliefs and values identified in the first exercise with those that emerge from the second is one way of uncovering contradictions. Our leadership stories are excellent reflections of our beliefs and values in action. When we are acting, we generally don't consciously recall beliefs and values that fit a given situation. Fundamental beliefs and values, the compasses for our action, are deep within us. We can recall many of them when asked. But when we are in an action situation, we don't have time to take a mental survey to ask, "What do I believe about this? What values relate to what I am doing now?" Thus our leadership stories are excellent representations of our beliefs and values in action.

Identifying Espoused Beliefs and Values. Espoused beliefs and values are those that we think we hold or think we ought to hold. One approach for identifying espoused beliefs and values is to draw a line down the center of a blank page. On the left side, create two columns, one headed "I believe," the other, "I feel"; on the right side, create two columns, one for "I value," the other for "I feel." (See Figure 5.1.) We could also be more systematic and add heads

Figure 5.1. My Beliefs and Values About Leadership.

I believe	*I feel*	*I value*	*I feel*

Sounds like a lot of work!

for the value and belief categories: reality-people, knowledge, ethics-aesthetics, leader qualities and characteristics, leadership approaches, expected outcomes of leadership, and educational perspectives (see Chapter Four).

Then fill in the columns. For instance, in the category "leader qualities and characteristics" one could write, "Leaders must be teachers and learners"; in the feeling column one might then write, "I am frustrated because leaders are generally associated only with power, not with teaching and learning"; in the values column one might write, "I value learning highly" and "I feel very good when I am learning."

Identifying Beliefs and Values in Action. Writing a story about a recent incident is a way of uncovering beliefs and values that guide our actions. Our beliefs and values in action may or may not be the same beliefs and values that we *say* guide our actions (our espoused beliefs and values). Thus writing a leadership story is one way to reveal contradictions between our espoused beliefs and values and our beliefs and values in action.

In no more than a page or two, write a description of an event (refer to Chapter Ten for a more complete description of this process). Be sure to give details: (1) When and where did the event occur? (2) What was the context for the event? Did something lead up it? If so, what? Was the event a surprise to you, or had you seen it coming? (3) Who were the people involved (not names but roles or positions)? What did each of them do? (4) What key dimensions of the event made it particularly pleasurable or particularly troublesome for you? Why? (5) Exactly how did you respond to the event? What did you do immediately? What did you do later? Once you have written your leadership story, you are ready to uncover some of your beliefs and values in action.

Let's examine a typical critical incident written by a departmental chair at a university and then attempt to discover some of this leader's beliefs and values.

As departmental chair, I recall an event about four months ago when a member of the department was scheduled for promotion to associate professor with tenure. The department had voted unanimously for the promotion, and the promotion materials were sent to the dean's advisory committee for approval. To the surprise of everyone in the department, the dean's advisory committee turned down the request for promotion.

When I heard of the advisory committee's negative vote, I was outraged. I called a special meeting of the department's faculty to design a strategy for appealing the decision. I was pleased to find the department once again solidly behind the staff member, with individual staff members volunteering to assist in the preparation of appeal material. I vowed to pull all the stops in confronting the advisory committee, firmly believing that my confrontation skills were as good as those of anyone on the committee.

On the day of the appeal (I was to appear in person to make the case), I dressed in my conservative navy blue suit. I rehearsed my short speech several times during the days before the meeting. On that day, I took my place at the end of the table, with twelve committee members staring at me. I had learned that the original vote had been ten to two, so I knew that two members of the committee were on my side, but I didn't know who they were.

I gave my presentation. They asked a few questions, and I was dismissed. Somehow I had expected more. I had expected, I guess, an opportunity to point out to them how dumb they had been in voting as they did the first time. It was probably a good thing that I hadn't had that opportunity.

A short while later I learned that the new vote had been seven in favor, five opposed. A positive recommendation for promotion would go forward to the dean. The department's staff member would be promoted to associate professor.

Let's examine the critical incident. What are some of the beliefs this administrative leader holds? It is clear that we can't begin to identify all of this person's beliefs from one brief critical incident statement. On the other hand, we can obtain some preliminary information. Here is one attempt.

Judging from his actions, this person holds the following beliefs:

My personal communication and confrontational skills are strong.

I am able to perform well in a stressful situation.

Image (manner of dress) is important.

Expressing emotion (outrage) is appropriate for a leader.

Leaders are human beings with emotions and feelings.

Leaders must display strength.

Leaders are in charge.

Leaders represent their group.

A group depends on its leader.

The group would accomplish little without a leader.

Leadership results in winners and losers.

An outcome of leadership is a solidified and supportive group.

Good leadership means attacking and solving emerging problems as quickly and efficiently as possible.

Confrontation is a powerful approach to resolving differences.

Getting the support of followers enhances a leader's power in times of confrontation.

Ends are more important than means—whatever approach it takes to winning a confrontation is the appropriate approach.

Judging from the brief account of the incident (note that it is more difficult to derive values from such an account than it is to identify beliefs), the following are things that this administrative leader values:

The people for whom I have administrative responsibility

The system and its approach to decision making (he did not question that an advisory committee makes decisions)

Justice (he believes that the staff person didn't receive a proper hearing by the advisory committee)

Searching for Sources of Beliefs and Values

Individuals and organizations obtain their beliefs and values from their histories, from present activities, and from the dominant paradigm of the society in which they exist.

As individuals, we are our histories. Many of our fundamental values about right and wrong, about people and how to relate to them, about organizations and institutions, about people different from us, and about other cultures and places in the world came to us during our growing-up years. The most powerful and profound beliefs and values we hold came from an often muddled past, frequently without our ever being aware of them.

The beliefs and values of society's dominant paradigm are yet another powerful influencer of organizational and individual beliefs and values. The values and beliefs of the dominant societal paradigm are so deeply embedded in organizations and people that many of them are hidden. Ferguson (1980), Capra (1983), and others have listed elements of the dominant societal paradigm: specialization is essential, efficiency—doing more with less—is always desirable, knowledge must be focused, the ultimate purpose of education is to provide for a career, accumulation of material goods equals success, time is linear, change is incremental, society is made up of individuals pursuing their own interests, and the role of institutions and governments is to enhance this purpose for individuals. (I have discussed these characteristics in an earlier work; see Apps, 1985, pp. 122–128.)

The following beliefs constitute the dominant paradigm for much of education: content is paramount, organized by discipline into courses; education involves acquiring a body of information or learning a skill; teaching means transferring information from teacher to learner; courses, workshops, or conferences are offered at the convenience of the instructors and presenters and the institution; and the instructors and presenters and the institution know best what a student should learn; quality is ensured by employing instructors and presenters with good credentials; and quality is ensured by offering credit courses in semester-long formats in classrooms in which students have an opportunity to compete for grades and from which learners with "deficiencies" are excluded.

Seldom are these beliefs and values discussed. For much of education they continue as the dominant paradigm. But as I explained in Chapter Two, we are on the threshold of the emerging age. This new paradigm will influence adult education organizations and its leadership in ways we cannot yet imagine.

changed a lot since then!

Adt Ed
Dist Ed
on-line learning

Examining Beliefs and Values

Once we have begun to uncover our beliefs and values, although interesting and probably revealing, we must do some additional work. We have already discussed the need to examine contradictions between our espoused beliefs and values and our beliefs and values in action. We must also compare our beliefs and values to those held by the organization in which we work. All leadership occurs in a context, and an important part of the context is the organization or institution that employs us.

We must also compare our beliefs and values within the context of the emerging age. For instance, let us return to the departmental chair we discussed earlier and compare some of his beliefs and values with those suggested by the emerging age.

- *"No argument with the context of the emerging age."* The new leader for adult education is clearly a whole person with mind, body, spirit and certainly emotions and feelings.
- *"Leaders are in charge"* and *"a group depends on its leader."* The emerging age suggests that these are obsolete beliefs. Leaders for the emerging age will learn to share power and responsibility within their organizations so that everyone participates in the organizational goals and large groups of people are not dependent on one or a few people for direction.
- *"Leadership results in winners and losers."* This is also an obsolete belief for advocates of a new approach for adult education leadership. For the emerging age, leadership involves collaboration and relationships more than competition and confrontation, which is implied by winning and losing.
- *"Ends are more important than means."* For the emerging age, both means (leadership approaches) and ends (the results of leadership) are important.

Now let's turn to the example of a leader who, upon examining her beliefs and values, finds them in conflict with those of her organization.

A particular adult education organization is committed to providing educational opportunities for minority groups, for women, and for people who are often reluctant to participate in educational programs. A newly employed administrative leader realizes after a few weeks on the job that many of her beliefs and values are in conflict with her organization's. She has many questions and concerns about programming as broadly as this organization wants. Furthermore, this leader believes that education ought to be provided for people who can best make use of it, not for those who may be reluctant learners or have shunned earlier opportunities to learn. Reflecting on her value statements, the leader realizes that she <u>values education so highly that she doesn't want to see it diluted</u>—which she believes would be the case if she tried to program for a broader audience.

The leader has several decisions to make. She can continue to believe as she does, and if she is true to her beliefs, she will probably find employment where concern for diversity is not as important as it is for this educational organization. She can hold her beliefs quietly and privately, not revealing them, and do what is politically correct to retain her job. That means that she would make a conscious decision to act in a way that contradicts her beliefs. A third option might be to set aside her old beliefs about education and replace them with beliefs that are more consistent with her organization's. I suspect that a fourth course might be for the leader to try to convince the organization that its beliefs and values about diversity are inappropriate and ought to be changed.

I have made all of this sound extremely logical and matter-of-fact, though <u>the process never is</u>. Whenever beliefs and values are involved, feelings are involved. Not only do we believe and value things at some level that we can describe and communicate, but we also hold deep feelings about our beliefs and values that are far less easy to communicate. Anger, frustration, sadness, pain, joy, and elation are often associated with our beliefs and values, particularly when they conflict with those of our organization, our community, or our friends.

Transformation Process

Like so many dimensions of leadership development, defining, searching for contradictions, and examining our beliefs and values is a transformation process (see Chapter Eleven). As we begin identifying and naming our beliefs and values and then compare our espoused beliefs and values with our actions, we usually reach a new *awareness* (the first phase of transformation). Upon searching more deeply for sources of our beliefs and values, and the feelings associated with what we have found, we experience one level of *analysis*. Through comparison of our beliefs and values with the context in which we work, the beliefs and values of our organization, and the requirements of the emerging age, we may be confronted with several *alternatives*.

Transition and decision occur when we decide which beliefs and values we wish to keep and which we wish to leave behind. We celebrate bringing forth old beliefs and values that fit our context, and we grieve leaving behind beliefs and values that we have decided are no longer appropriate. We take *action* on our revised beliefs and values, and this may send us back to any of the earlier phases of the transformation process.

The foregoing description is of course simplistic. The process of identifying, examining, and making decisions about our own beliefs and values is usually heart-wrenching and extremely challenging. Whenever we examine and try to make sense of the most fundamental dimensions of who we are, it is never easy to explain in some quick set of phases. Yet the transformation process can help us understand what we are thinking and feeling when we wrestle with our beliefs and values.

Beliefs, Values, and Leaders for the Emerging Age

The process suggested here is one of examination and appraisal. I have argued that leaders benefit by knowing what they believe and value about leadership and about themselves as people and as leaders. I do not want to leave the impression that all values and beliefs must be relevant to the context in which the leader works and thus all of leadership is situational. I maintain that certain values and beliefs transcend context. I would even go so far as to say that if a certain context makes it difficult for the leader to express these transcendent beliefs and values, the context likely needs changing.

What values transcend context? How far can we go in discussing "universal" values? Some people would argue that universal values are universal only insofar as a given culture is concerned. When we move to another culture (to work in another country, for example), we discover that few values transcend cultures. Some people would argue that at the most fundamental level we include such values as survival and concern for protecting offspring. Many argue that rights to housing, food, health care, and other basics transcend time and place. And Sperry (1981) and others argue that unless we value care for the environment, no other values matter. But beyond this level of values, few, if any, transcend cultures. Many people in the United States argue that such values as justice, honesty, love for family, and so on are universal values and ought to be promoted around the globe. Other cultures have other ideas about what values are universal. It is not my purpose here to discuss global values in conflict, but it is often the case that when disagreements and misunderstandings occur in negotiations, they can be traced to fundamental differences in beliefs and values.

Understanding the beliefs and values we hold is fundamental to developing a philosophy of leadership. In the next four chapters we will begin examining in some depth further elements of a personal philosophy of leadership, beginning with leader qualities and characteristics.

Chapter Six

Qualities and Characteristics of the New Leaders

The emerging age will require adult education leaders with particular qualities and characteristics, some of which have not been popular or even known in the past. In developing a personal philosophy of leadership (see Chapter Five), understanding leader qualities and characteristics is a key component, along with expected leadership outcomes, leadership approaches, and educational perspectives.

It is extremely important to note that not all of the qualities and characteristics described here will fit every leadership context. That is why in developing a leadership philosophy, studying the context must be the first step. It is also important to recognize that the leadership needed in this emerging age is concerned with communications and relationships, not solo performance. Even though we are discussing leadership qualities and characteristics, we cannot lose sight of the fact that leadership, in addition to being in context, is always in relationship to other people.

Picture Yourself as a Leader

One of the first things I ask participants in my leadership workshops is to draw a picture that reflects how they see themselves as leaders. This is usually greeted by some shuffling of feet and mild protests. I explain that drawing a picture is a powerful way to communicate who we are. As I distribute large sheets of paper (usually newsprint pages from flip charts) and some felt-tipped pens of various colors, I point out that as highly verbal people, we are able to discuss who we are as leaders quite easily, but drawing ourselves as leaders is often more of a challenge.

By this time I am hearing more protests: "Isn't this something that kids ordinarily do?"

"Yes, it is," I answer.

"But I have never been very good at drawing."

"That doesn't matter; most people aren't very good at drawing."

Participants become resolved to the fact that they will have to draw something. The protests cease, and concern shifts to mechanics. I state that the only rule is that they may use no words in their drawings. I go on to explain that by drawing a picture, we are able to reveal something of who we are as leaders that may not have been thought of or put into words. I then suggest that participants go off to a corner of the room and work on their drawings. This elicits considerable furrowing of brows, shuffling of paper, and delaying tactics such as searching for just the right colors of marking pens.

Participants look out of the corner of their eyes at what their colleagues are drawing; some make preliminary sketches on a smaller sheet of paper—blueprints for what they plan to draw on the larger sheet. I allow twenty to thirty minutes for the group to draw the pictures, which are really metaphors for each person's self-image as a leader. When they are done, we tape the pictures to the wall. I encourage people who finish early to walk around and look at the other people's drawing, reflecting silently on what they see.

When all drawings are up on the wall, I ask each person to say a few words about his or her drawing. Participants are also encouraged to ask questions. By the time we have made it around the room, the participants are impressed by a variety of observations: that the quality of the artistic effort doesn't matter in creating a picture, that group members' views of themselves as leaders are widely divergent, and that some people simply can't face drawing a picture of themselves as a leader and so instead draw a picture that depicts some general process of leadership.

I leave the pictures on the wall. Toward the end of the workshop, I encourage the participants to consider how they might now draw their pictures differently.

Draw Your Own Picture

Get yourself a large sheet of paper and marking pens or crayons in a variety of colors. (Bold, colorful lines add an important dimension to your drawing.) Draw yourself as a leader. When you have finished, hang the drawing above your desk and look at it from time to time to see how you might change it. If you have a friend who is interested in learning more about new approaches to leadership, do your drawings together at a prearranged time and then share the drawings with each other. Feedback from another person—questions asked and comments made—can give you a perspective on your drawing that you might not have thought of yourself.

You might find it interesting to compare your picture (metaphor) with those that other leaders have drawn. In one workshop, a dean from a northern city drew a picture of a snowplow. Describing his picture, he said that he spent much of his time clearing a path so that others could do their work. He said that he was the point man in their organization and that often the snow was deep and drifted but he needed to venture forth, clearing the way so that others could do their jobs more easily.

Another administrator drew a picture of a soccer coach. She said she saw herself standing on the sidelines, trying to figure out strategies to follow, becoming acquainted with the competition, following the rules, and constantly encouraging her team to win.

Several workshop participants have drawn pictures depicting a journey. One drew a winding trail that crossed over treacherous ground, passed by spectacular scenery, encountered land mines and shaky bridges, sometimes experienced a smoothly paved thoroughfare, other times a rutted, stony path. Sometimes the track wasn't visible at all and the leader had to hack out a trail. Another drew a picture of a person climbing a mountain enshrouded in fog with a poorly defined footpath to the top. This person, explaining her drawing, said that when the leader burst through the clouds and achieved what she thought was the top of the mountain, she saw yet another mountain in the distance to climb, except this one seemed to have no trail at all, and at first glance appeared impossible to climb.

Leader Metaphors

As I have watched many leaders in action over the years, several metaphors have come to mind. For example, early one morning, my wife and I were out walking on a little-traveled mountain road. Ahead of us I heard "rat-tat-tat," again and again. I was curious as to what or who was violating the early-morning quiet in the mountains. Then ahead of us I saw a yellow metal road sign, and sitting on the top of it was a woodpecker, pounding away on the sign with all its might. That woodpecker reminded me of some leaders I have known—they make loud noises at all hours, but they seem to accomplish little beyond the "rat-tat-tat" of their voices breaking the silence.

I have seen leaders that reminded me of warriors. They saw their role as defining an enemy and then attempting to destroy it at all costs. Their style was confrontational; their goal was to win. Losing was a disgrace. They spent their careers defining enemies and then scheming how to confront and beat them in battle. Most disconcerting to the warrior-leader were those persons who didn't want to fight but, rather, sought solutions that would leave multiple winners.

The politician is a common metaphor for many leaders I have known. They work hard to develop networks of people in high places that they can call on when the going gets tough. For them, whom you know is far more important than what you know. They spend much of their time developing relationships with people who they believe can assist them or whose support they believe they need to survive. Many politicians are aboveboard, honest, and ethical. But some believe that to be effective, a politician must withhold information, twist facts, and stir up conflict.

The leader as facilitator brings people together, finds resources, searches for information, and then steps back, allowing the process to work. The facilitator often has no vision or direction in mind. Such a leader believes that the group will decide on its vision and direction in due course and that the leader's role is to support the decision-making process.

The white knight in shining armor is something like the woodpecker—lots of style but little substance. The white knight enjoys the position of leader and works to make sure everyone knows who is the boss. Occasionally, when serious problems erupt in the organization, the white knight likes to wait until zero hour and then come charging heroically in to solve the problem.

The paternalist, a fairly common leader in many organizations, genuinely cares about the members of the organization and the organization itself. The paternalist sees the organization as a family and its employees as family members. As leader, the paternalist is the family head and thus responsible for everything that the family does, as a unit and individually.

Strivers work exceedingly hard. They put in long hours and often go well beyond what is expected of them. The motivation for the striver's hard work is personal gain and advancement. Each position held is viewed as a steppingstone to some higher position. The current leadership position is but a temporary stopping place on the journey upward. Unfortunately for many strivers, they wear their ambition on their shirtsleeve and may be turned down for advancement because of it.

A few tyrants may be found in organizations, though usually not in top positions anymore. The tyrant rules by threat and intimidation. In the army I served under commanders who were tyrants. Their orders were followed under threat of punishment if not carried out exactly as issued. Tyrants suspect everyone of being lazy, stupid, and intent on finding ways of getting around them. (This last suspicion is probably fairly accurate!)

The academic leader, still often found in educational organizations, is a person who has probably had some success as a teacher or as a researcher and is then appointed to an administrative post. Academic leaders often try to lead as they have been taught or as they have conducted research. They try to keep everything "objective" as they bring voluminous amounts of research and data to leadership problems. They see the employees in the organization as their students and sometimes wonder why these students are not carrying out their assignments exactly as the leader expected. Some academic leaders become excellent administrators after considerable on-the-job learning and study. Others start out failing as leaders and continue failing, returning to their academic posts disillusioned and baffled by the meaning of organizational leadership.

As an orchestra conductor brings together a group of people with different specialties, so does the leader bring together vastly different people. As the orchestra conductor keeps everyone playing the same tune, each contributing to making the whole much more than the sum of the parts, so does the leader.

If we envision leadership as moving toward some vision to be reached, journey guide is an appropriate metaphor for the leader. The journey guide helps keep the party on the path, moving always toward the goal to be achieved. Members of the party may all contribute to the trip, some responsible for carrying the gear, some for preparing food, and so on. But overall, the journey guide keeps everyone on course and moving forward.

Robert Greenleaf (1977) writes about the leader as servant, in service to the people and the organization for whom the leader has responsibility. In some ways this metaphor is the opposite of more traditional ideas about the leader in charge and in control in that the leaders serve the people who have selected them to lead.

Which metaphors of all of these mentioned are consistent with the challenges of the emerging age—concerns for context and change, for support rather than control, for artistry as well as science, for capacity as well as competency? A few come close. The leader as snowplow is more interested in support than in control. The mountain climber expresses well the experience for many adult education leaders trying to lead in new ways. The leader as orchestra conductor, although having elements of control, certainly represents a situation in which many adult education administrators find themselves. The journey guide and servant fit many leaders who are trying to be consistent with the assumptions of the emerging age.

I would like to add yet one more metaphor that I believe fits the requirements of the emerging age: the leader as daisy.

As I mentioned earlier, the metaphor for adult education leadership in the emerging age that makes sense to me is of a living organism rather than a machine. The daisy is influenced greatly by its environment, the soil in which it grows, the amount of moisture present, the hours of sunlight, and the extent of competition from other plants. But the daisy also gives back. Its roots hold the soil from erosion. Its vegetation, at season's end, adds nutrients to the soil. For passersby it provides a flash of color, often in the midst of otherwise drab surroundings. Daisies are known for their ability to grow in difficult places—along railroad rights-of-way, in the little islands of busy intersections, and on the median strips of major highways. A daisy is known for its resiliency. An animal walks by and plucks off the petals or perhaps consumes the entire plant, a chattering mower slices off an entire hillside of the colorful flowers, a spell of dry weather challenges the daisy's life—under all these conditions, the daisy continues to grow, shooting up another stem if one is removed, continuing to thrive even if conditions are less than satisfactory.

The daisy and contemporary leaders are alike in many ways. Leaders may be removed from an assignment from time to time, have resources decreased or eliminated, and face adversity from many quarters. But leaders, like the resilient daisy, continue their work, providing little splashes of color in a sometimes harsh or drab world. They experience the influences of their environment, but, like the daisy, they constantly try to make a difference as well. They attempt to influence as well as be influenced. They are proactive and reactive, often, it seems, at the same time.

Thus the metaphor of a daisy can help us understand, at a level that suggests understanding beyond words, what leaders for the emerging age are about. Metaphors often evoke feelings and emotions as well as word images. An important characteristic of leaders and leadership for the emerging age goes well beyond words into the realm of feelings and emotions that often can't be expressed well verbally but require pictures and other images for communication. The picture of a daisy helps me begin to understand leaders and leadership beyond the dimensions of the mind, into deeper levels of understanding. Those dimensions of leadership, not easily described in words but expressed in the practice of leadership, often make all the difference.

Leader Qualities and Characteristics

Adult education leaders in the emerging age will have to exhibit a wide variety of qualities and characteristics. We will discuss some of the most important of them here.

Passion

Leaders for the emerging age are passionate about what they do and how they do it. Passion goes beyond motivation and commitment. Passion comes from the core of what leaders value and believe. Passion keeps leaders moving toward a goal even when everything seems to go wrong. Passion keeps them committed to what they believe is important when others choose to move on.

Rich Crandall (1993) says, "Whatever approach you take, you must find your passion. If you can't find it right away, do something that feels right to you so your passion can develop" (p. 5). Passion, like spirit, is a fundamental quality for leaders, particularly for those who are committed to new directions for adult education organizations.

Awareness of Personal History

Each of us is influenced by our past. How we think, what we think, how we learn, what we learn, even what we see and do not see is a product of our histories. We don't see things as *they* are but rather as *we* are. Thus it is critical for leaders to be aware of their personal history. That is not to say that history alone determines our present behavior. As we become aware of our histories—and thus come to know another side of ourselves—we can in many instances make a conscious decision to override them. We cannot rewrite our histories, but we can change our responses to them and even their meaning. (Guidelines for exploring personal histories are presented in Chapter Ten.)

Spirituality

In Chapter Four we discussed the spiritual dimension of leaders. Each of us has a spiritual side, whether we wish to acknowledge it or not. We may use different words to describe it. We may talk about our soul or the heart of our being. We may discuss a power outside of ourselves to which we relate. Whatever we call it, our spiritual side is the most fundamental aspect of who we are. Our spirituality goes beyond credentials and experience, beyond skills and knowledge. Our spiritual side guides us, at the deepest levels of our being, as to who we are, what we do, and how we do it.

Balance

Adult education leaders for the emerging age balance their family and personal life with their work life. They refuse to accept the premise of some organizations that leaders must devote their lives to the organization, working sixty-hour weeks or more and never for a moment letting the organization out of their mind. Leaders have outside interests; they go on vacations; they need time for solitude; they take sabbaticals to study and renew themselves. Leaders have a deeply united sense of body, mind, and spirit and an integrated sense of past, present, and future. They know history well but are keenly aware of the present and the challenges of the future. They are also able to recognize the symptoms of burnout and take steps to avoid it.

Leaders for the emerging age also strive for balance in their work goals, recognizing the learning needs of individuals but also accepting family, organizational, and societal needs. Marie Kerpan (1993) writes, "One aspect of balancing is the need to temper the race for wealth and power with the higher values of a civilized society, such as integrity, prudence, compassion, and authenticity" (p. 3).

Skills

As described in Chapter Three, leaders rely on such skills as creative and critical thinking, communicating, relating to people, reflecting on activities, and framing questions in often ambiguous and chaotic situations. As important as these skills are, perhaps the most critical one of all is the ability to develop new skills, sometimes as they are practiced. Expert carpenters, encountering a situation for which they do not have a tool, may create a tool on the spot. Expert carpenters are thus not only tool users but also tool makers. Leaders increasingly need to invent new tools (skills) rather than depend on the old ones in their tool (skill) box. Many leader skills in the leader's skill box remain there, for they do not fit current leadership situations. Leaders continually make decisions about whether a current skill fits or whether a new skill is called for. Abandoning a tried-and-true old skill for an untried new one takes courage. But it is far more dangerous to attempt to use old skills in new situations where they simply aren't appropriate. I'm reminded of the old story of the man who knew how to use a hammer well and so came to every situation believing that his hammering skills were the appropriate ones. We've all known leaders like this.

Many adult education leaders these days are in organizations, especially ones funded with tax dollars, that are under pressure to become smaller. These leaders have experience in helping organizations redirect their efforts to accommodate growth and expansion; few have had that sort of experience in organizations that are shrinking. Hence many leaders, facing budget cuts, staff layoffs, and redirection of programming, have no blueprints to follow. They are developing the skills for helping organizations become smaller as they are practicing them. Many are trying to follow their fundamental values and beliefs about fairness, humane treatment of individuals, and concern for the public that is served. These elements of their leadership philosophies provide a foundation for what they do and how they do it. But the actual skills they have to practice in making the cuts and redirecting the programs are discovered in the doing of them.

For some of these leaders, budget cuts and their implications came with little warning. They came as unexpected changes, or what Charles Handy (1989) calls discontinuous change. Discontinuous change almost always requires the invention of new skills.

Solitude and Contemplation

Leaders understand the power of solitude and contemplation in reflecting on who they are, where they are, what they are doing, why they are doing it, and where their organization is going. They seek out times to be alone and to confront themselves at deeper and more profound levels. Contemporary society encourages busyness and togetherness. Leaders know that busyness without solid thought and direction often leads nowhere.

Anthony Storr (1988) takes the need for solitude further. "It appears . . . that some development of the capacity to be alone is necessary if the brain is to function at its best, and if the individual is to fulfill his [or her] highest potential. Human beings easily become alienated from their own deepest needs and feelings. Learning, thinking, innovation and maintaining contact with one's own inner world are all facilitated by solitude" (p. 28) (see Chapter Ten).

Tolerance for Paradox

As perplexing as paradox often is, leaders learn to become comfortable with it. Paradox can be defined as a statement or situation that seems unbelievable, contradictory, or even absurd, but in fact may be true. Leaders know that human nature itself is filled with paradoxes (for example, everything is simple and everything is complex, our weaknesses are our strengths and our strengths are our weaknesses).

Tom Peters (1987) says that the core paradox "that all leaders at all levels must contend with is fostering internal stability in order to encourage the pursuit of constant change" (p. 395). He goes on to say that having a well-defined organizational vision is necessary for an organization to take constant risks. The same paradox exists for the leader as a person. I would restate Peters's comment: the adult education leader for the emerging age must be internally stable (have a well-developed philosophy of leadership) so as to adjust to and stimulate change constantly.

Leaders face many other paradoxes. Janet Hagberg (1984, p. 134) lists the following as examples of paradoxes leaders face:

The more we know the less we know.

Continuity is change.

The question is the answer.

Evil and good are siblings.

Our strength is our weakness, and our weakness is our strength.

Other examples of paradoxes leaders face include these:

We can take charge by letting go.

We gain power by giving it away. — *Jesus said this centuries ago*

One can lead and follow at the same time.

One must be able to move forward, backward, and sideways within a matter of moments.

Ends and means do not mix.

One cannot know the destination until the trip has begun.

Build on past leadership approaches by contradicting them.

Lead invisibly.

Start in the middle and work toward the beginning.

Doing less is doing more.

What is soft is strong.

As we discipline ourselves, we become more free. *Jesus said this centuries ago, too.*

Courage

It takes courage to be an administrative leader in adult education these days. That's easy to say but difficult for many leaders to do. Courage means doing what you believe is the right thing to do. Courage means following your personal credo; it means working toward an organizational vision that others may fault. Courage often means taking a longer-term view and accepting the short-term consequences.

Courage means backbone and strength. It means persistence and patience and sometimes the need to do nothing, to step out of the way. Being courageous means not pleasing everyone; at times it may seem that no one is pleased with what you are doing—not until after it is done and people begin to see the wisdom of it all.

Part of being courageous is willingness to take risks. Risk taking, by definition, involves failure from time to time, and failure is not a positive concept in our society. Our society puts tremendous pressure on people to succeed. The pressure to succeed is so great for many people that their self-worth is determined largely by their success. The extreme pressure put on people to succeed at all cost creates a tremendous fear of failure.

For fear of failing, many leaders avoid striking out into new areas. They do everything possible to avoid risk taking. For the emerging age, risk taking is absolutely essential. Leaders must accept the fact that because they often will be drawing up the blueprints for their actions while they act, they are bound to fail some of the time.

You may be familiar with the following story, but it bears repeating. Thomas Edison was aware of Humphrey Davy's 1808 experiments that resulted in producing a brilliant arc of light four inches long when two pieces of charcoal were brought near each other and connected to a battery. He knew that arc lights had been used in 1844 to light a production of the Paris Opera. The carbon in these lights was consumed in the process of lighting.

Edison wanted to create something more substantial—an electric light that could be self-contained and could be turned on and off many times before it required replacement. Edison was aware of scientific research that had been done with electricity. But the mathematics of electricity was beyond him. "I do not depend on figures at all," he admitted. "I try an experiment and reason out the result, somehow, by methods which I could not explain" (Conot, 1979, p. 132).

Edison also recalled, "At the time I experimented on the incandescent lamp I did not understand Ohm's Law. It would prevent me from experimenting" (p. 133). On one occasion, in 1879, Edison invited several of his investors to a demonstration of his light bulb experiments. Sixteen bulbs were illuminated, but within a few seconds, sparks began flying from each bulb. Then one bulb shone more brightly than the rest before it exploded with a loud crack, sending shards of glass everywhere. Soon another bulb blew up, and then another. End of demonstration. After thirteen months of experiments, encountering failure after failure, Edison began to have doubts that a commercial incandescent light bulb was possible. But the 260th version, with a horseshoe filament, worked. The world would be forever changed. Failure after failure after failure finally led to success. But were they really failures? Or were they steppingstones, risk-taking events necessary for success?

Courage is not something to strive for or study for. But it can be learned by watching and emulating people who exhibit it.

The director of cooperative extension for a state with an expanding urban population and a declining rural population, set out with his staff and appropriate planning committees to redirect extension programming with more emphasis on urban youth at risk and with concern for nutrition programs for low-income people. Resources previously used for agricultural production programs were to be diverted for this use. Lawmakers were generally supportive of the changed program direction; in fact, many of the urban legislators had encouraged the shift. As expected, agricultural organizations, commodity groups, animal breed organizations, and the like were furious, particularly with the program director. They pointed out that cooperative extension programs were initially created to help agriculture, not to deal with urban problems. Even though agricultural producers represented only a fraction of the state's growing population, they insisted that they were being shortchanged and that the director would someday regret supporting the program change.

The director got many phone calls at work and at home, some late at night. He received a barrage of letters. He continued to support the program shifts, at the same time not eliminating agricultural programming. Now, many months later, the organization's program direction has shifted, and several successful programs are in progress in the urban areas. The agricultural groups' general unhappiness remains, but they have come to understand why the decisions were made as they were, and most of them have a new respect for the director even though many of them did not agree with his decisions.

With all the pressure on this director, it would have been easy to cave in to the agricultural groups. But he stayed with the organization's decision. That's a clear display of courage.

Perspective

In a graduate course I teach, the majority of the students work as administrative leaders in a variety of adult and continuing education organizations. Most of them are working full time and studying part time. For one project, I ask them to describe the broad field of adult education and then look at where they think it is headed and where they think their organization fits.

Most of them have a difficult time with this assignment. They know their own organization quite well, but beyond that their knowledge is limited. Also, many of them question the value of looking beyond their own organization. Leaders for the emerging age are aware not only of their own organization and where it is headed but also of the broader field of adult education and people-serving organizations. And they are very clear as to how their organization fits into the bigger picture.

As part of a leadership development program for middle managers, we went to central Alabama, visiting and living with African-American families. One day we visited with a black community development leader who was talking about some of the problems faced by people living in this area.

One member of our group held up her hand midway through the presentation. "It seems to me this is what you ought to consider doing," she began. She went on to outline a series of steps she had followed when doing community development work in a midwestern state.

Our host was polite but obviously upset by this off-the-cuff analysis of the situation in his community. "Sometimes you have to walk awhile in another person's shoes before you can begin to understand that person's problems," he said. He was talking about multiple perspectives and the need to stop and realize that problems may look one way through our eyes but quite different through the eyes of the people who are actually experiencing the problems.

Adult education leaders must become students of the context in which they live and work (see Chapter Four for an in-depth discussion). As leaders try to understand their organization and the broader context of their community, they must rope off their personal histories and experiences and allow themselves to learn this special context. If they do not rope off their personal histories, their cultural perspective will interfere with what they wish to come to know.

Earlier, when I discussed becoming aware of our own personal histories, I talked about the danger of seeing things not as *they* are but as *we* are. This is particularly relevant as we try to learn about our organizations and communities as unique entities with their own unique contexts.

Although certain general leadership skills transcend contexts, many such skills are context specific. A leadership strategy that works well in one organizational context may not work at all in another. This is not to say that an organization's context is frozen and unchanging; far from it. The way in which an organization changes may be one important part of its context. It is often chal-

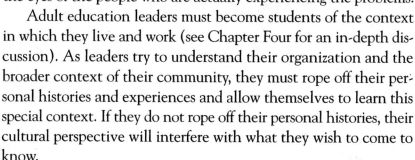

lenging for both the leaders and the organization when a new administrator is hired from outside. Leaders, attempting to understand the organization's context and fit within it, try to avoid compromising their beliefs and values. Thus we sometimes see leader beliefs and values in conflict with organizational beliefs and values. In many situations, both leaders and organizations benefit from this exchange. In too many situations, leaders find that they cannot compromise their own beliefs and values, and they move on.

In the next chapter we begin exploring another dimension of a personal philosophy of leadership: leadership outcomes.

Chapter Seven

Redefining Leadership Expectations and Outcomes

While developing a personal philosophy of leadership, adult education leaders must wrestle with the question of what they expect to happen as the result of their leadership efforts. They must examine the outcome expectations of their organization, but they must also examine the leadership outcomes associated with the emerging age.

Leadership in the emerging age focuses on both process and product, on how leadership is done and what results from the effort. Obviously, one set of outcomes of leadership efforts finds the adult education organization doing what it says it will do and doing it well. Beyond carrying out its stated purposes, other outcomes reasonably expected include approaches for periodically examining vision, mission, and strategic plans; recognizing serendipity; collective spirituality; and organizational development and renewal.

Deciding on Organizational Purpose

An essential outcome for leadership is a clear statement of organizational purpose, accompanied by strategies for achieving that purpose. An organization's purpose is expressed in its vision or mission statement and its annual plan or other program plans.

Often missing from an organization's purpose is a vision—a far-reaching and inspirational statement that sets the tone, direction, and philosophy for the organization. Vision statements are generally incorporated into an organization's mission statement, which clearly spells out what the organization plans to do that is different from the programs of other adult and continuing education organizations in the community, as well as program approaches that it plans to use.

One clear responsibility of an adult education administrative leader is helping the organization decide on its purpose, particularly its vision and its mission. An organization's purpose is not merely a continuation of past activities, although many organizations view it that way. Once a vision and mission have been determined, they are not set in stone. They must be reviewed periodically, updated, and sometimes even abandoned to accommodate changing conditions.

A few years ago I was asked to help a university college determine its future direction. Several committees had met for some months, examining trend data, looking at available resources, and attempting to make decisions about the future direction of the unit's educational programs. One day while meeting with the dean, I suggested that we work on a mission statement for the college.

"Oh," he said, looking a bit puzzled. "I believe we have one of those around here someplace."

He buzzed his secretary and asked her to bring in the mission statement. He sorted through the pages for a minute or so. "Here are several mission statements, Jerry; pick out one you like and we'll use it."

Unfortunately, this attitude toward mission statements is not unusual among administrative leaders. They have been told that mission statements are necessary, but the leaders don't see them as having any importance.

Elements of an Educational Organization's Purpose

Before looking at the elements of purpose statements in more depth, let's examine some basic questions. Are there values in an adult education organization's purpose statement that ought to be similar for all organizations, agencies, and groups? Other values could be mentioned, but I believe that all adult education organizations ought to be committed to accessibility, responsiveness, relevance to people and the community, programs that challenge participants, respect for learners, and the highest possible quality of offerings.

- Accessibility means creating conditions that make it easier for adult learners to participate. This may mean reexamining offerings to take into account people who can't attend classes, workshops, and conferences during daytime hours. It may mean making some offerings available via educational media, such as interactive computers, so that people can study at their own pace, at their own place, and at the times they select. It means making educational sites accessible to people with disabilities of various kinds. And it means having a fee schedule that will allow the largest number to participate. Sometimes accessibility may mean providing scholarships for people who are unable to pay. For instance, I teach a writing workshop that makes several hundred dollars in scholarships available to students who may have writing ability but can't afford the fees.

- Responsiveness means making learning opportunities available when they are requested, not months or years later. Responsiveness must be tempered with reason and adherence to a mission statement—sometimes we are trapped into believing that we ought to try to respond to everyone.

- People want an institution's educational offerings to be relevant to their personal problems and challenges. This means that an educational institution must constantly update its offerings in light of changes in the community and the ever-evolving challenges faced by individuals.

- Challenging learners means helping participants move beyond where there are now, questioning their beliefs, perspectives, and opinions.

• Respecting learners means embracing diversity, providing a comfortable environment, and recognizing learners as fellow human beings on a learning journey. It includes providing an atmosphere that fosters good relationships between instructor and students, among students, and between students and knowledge sources.

• Quality includes moving beyond instructor credentials, the number of hours spent in class, and the difficulty of the examinations. Increasingly, quality is viewed as a combination of standards set by the organization *and* expectations from the participants for learning that is relevant, practical, challenging, and up-to-date.

What are some approaches for moving beyond these more universal goals? One is to develop an organizational vision.

Approaches to Vision Making

First, exactly what is a vision?* We hear the word bandied about regularly in conversation these days. Everyone, it seems, either is a visionary or wants to be one—and insists that everyone else ought to be one as well. Visions are important, for individuals as well as for organizations. A few years ago the buzz activity was the development of a mission statement—that was and is, in fact, an important activity for an organization.

Unfortunately such terms as *vision, mission,* and *strategic plan* become all tangled together. Let's begin with some sorting. First, let's look at vision. Tichy and Devanna (1986) say, "The vision is the ideal to strive for. It releases energy needed to motivate the organization to action. It provides an overarching framework to

---

*Portions of this discussion first appeared in Jerold W. Apps, "Beliefs, Values and Vision Making for Continuing Education," *Continuing Higher Education Review,* 1990, 54(3), 124–135.

guide day-to-day decisions and priorities and provides the parameters for [action]" (p. 126).

Peters (1987, pp. 401–404) lists eight characteristics of visions:

1. Effective visions are inspiring.
2. Effective visions are clear and challenging—and about excellence.
3. Effective visions make sense in the marketplace and, by
   stressing flexibility and execution, stand the test of time in a
   turbulent world.
4. Effective visions must be stable but constantly challenged—
   and changed at the margin.
5. Effective visions are beacons and controls when all else is up
   for grabs.
6. Effective visions are aimed at empowering our own people
   first, customers second.
7. Effective visions prepare for the future but honor the past.
8. Effective visions are lived in details, not broad strokes.

For me, a vision provides direction plus emotional appeal. It
tells people what they ought to strive for and also gives them a reason to do so. A vision statement is a road map and a dream combined. A vision simultaneously provokes passion and provides
parameters.

Vision making means creating a dream that is not a mere
extension of the past but is influenced by history and draws on it.
Vision making often means a transformation, leaving behind old
ideas and ways of doing things and moving forward into risky and
unexplored ways of thinking and doing. Developing a vision, a
dream for an organization, means confronting present programs and
structures, examining them, and then deciding to abandon, modify, or continue with them.

Vision making is also personal. Each of us, as human beings, has visions. In Chapter Four we discussed writing a personal credo statement, which is another way of describing a personal vision. Visions are not easy for people. "Most adults have little sense of real vision," says Senge (1990). "We have goals and objectives, but these are not visions. When asked what they want, many adults say what they want to get rid of" (p. 147). They have a kind of negative vision rather than a view of some ultimate positive desire.

Individuals have visions about their organizations as well. One responsibility, a challenge for the leader, is to strive for a shared vision. Shared vision means people coming to a shared understanding of the organization's direction as they reflect on, discuss, and work out a vision for the organization.

Conflict often exists between an individual's vision for an organization and the corporate or shared vision that a group of individuals develop. Within reason, such conflict can be healthy and worthwhile, because those who differ provide a mirror or a counterpoint that permits the group to examine its vision making in a new light.

Peters (1987) sums up the process of vision making well: "Visions come from within—as well as from outside. They are personal—and group centered. Developing a vision and values is a messy, artistic process" (p. 401).

An error too often made in organizations is for only the administrator, the department head, the dean, or the executive director to be permitted to have a vision. The administrator writes down the vision statement, publishes it in the organization's newsletter, gives copies to each staff person, and makes it available to stakeholders. Then the administrator sits back, waiting for good things to happen—and nothing does, except for some carping by those who read the statement and wonder what it means or wonder why they weren't asked to contribute to its development.

Vision making is too often accomplished in just this fashion. Such vision statements are little better than no vision statement at all. True, the administrator should be visionary and have a vision. But administrative leaders for the emerging age know that they must involve the entire organization in the process of developing the vision statement, as awkward and difficult as this process often is. A vision statement is worthless if it is not shared and does not come from the heart and soul of everyone in the organization. It is only then that people become committed to carrying out the vision.

The director of a large continuing education program was perceived by his colleagues as a person with vision for continuing education. He served on several national committees and helped write national vision statements for continuing education. He clearly knew where his own organization ought to be headed and how it should get there. At various staff meetings, he shared his vision with great commitment and passion. Everyone was impressed with his clarity of direction and his broad perspective. But unfortunately, only a minority of the staff agreed with him, and almost none of them had been involved in developing the organization's vision statement. Today this director works for another organization.

Vision statements for adult education organizations often include statements such as the following:

Striving for diversity of program offerings

Redefining teaching approaches in light of electronic media

Modifying teaching and learning strategies and taking into account differing social, ethnic, and racial situations

Considering all people, staff as well as participants, as human beings, not as numbers

Creating an organizational structure that allows each individual to make a maximum creative contribution

Developing a climate where power is shared so that employees can make authentic decisions about the conditions in their work environment

Of course, many vision statements are, as they should be, specific to a particular continuing education organization, reflecting its unique mission.

Mission Statements

Mission statements express what an organization is trying to accomplish, within certain parameters. As Peter Drucker (1992) aptly states in his discussion of leadership and nonprofit organizations, "The best nonprofits devote a great deal of thought to defining their organization's mission. They avoid sweeping statements full of good intention and focus, instead, on objectives that have clear-cut implications for the work their members perform—staff and volunteers both" (p. 205).

A mission statement helps define the niche within which a particular adult education organization fits. With many organizations seemingly competing with one another, a challenge is for each to define its niche. Mission includes language about the niche and what the organization hopes to accomplish within this niche. For example, here are several statements from the University of Wisconsin Extension mission statement:

We are a world-class organization of inspired university educators committed to helping people use knowledge to improve their lives. *We are committed to excellence* . . . in our faculty and staff and in our programs. Our excellence is founded on the scholarship behind the research and knowledge we share and on our unique ability to apply this knowledge to meet people's needs. *We are committed to people* . . . and to meeting their most important needs. We empower people with knowledge, attitudes, skills, and aspiration. *We are committed to partnerships* . . . among county, state and federal governments, between campus and county faculty and staff, between university people and volunteers and between public and private organizations. We recognize that the strength and durability of these partnerships rests on shared responsibility, shared concerns, shared authority, shared costs, and shared recognition. *We are committed to change* . . . in the direction and focus of our programs. As society and technology evolve, we direct our resources toward the most pressing needs of citizens and communities. *We are committed to openness* . . . both among ourselves and in our relationships with the public. We believe in being accountable and in meeting the test of vigorous public oversight. *We are committed to diversity* . . . because our differences enrich us. We embrace diversity in our faculty, staff and clientele, respect diversity of opinion and take pride in the diversity of our programs. *We are committed to accessibility* . . . and to extending the influence and expertise of the university to every corner of our state. Through our county-based faculty and staff, our campus specialists and our use of state-of-the-art technology, we bring the University of Wisconsin's research and knowledge within the reach of every citizen.

Drucker (1992) concludes, "A clearly defined mission will foster innovative ideas and help others understand why they need to be implemented—however much they fly in the face of tradition" (p. 207).

How do vision, mission, and plan relate? A vision provides a foundation for action—a global sense of direction that is based on individual and organizational beliefs and values. A mission is a specific direction statement, grounded within the vision, about what the organization is attempting to accomplish. A strategic or long-range plan is a specific set of directions for how a mission will be carried out.

Flexible Programming

Even with the best-laid plans, rapidly changing conditions require flexibility on the part of adult education administrators, teachers, and staff. Adult education organizations must have visions, missions, and action plans. But everyone who has worked in an adult education organization knows that the best-developed plans must sometimes be abandoned in order for the organization to respond to its participants and its community.

For instance, county extension agents have carefully developed plans of work. But when a flood hits their community, a rare disease infests a major crop, or a nearby military base closes, they adjust their plans to accommodate the new educational demands. A mission statement is of course essential at these times, for it serves as a guide for deciding which emerging problems should be worked on and which would best be addressed by someone else.

A criticism of some adult education organizations has been their slowness in responding to rapidly changing needs and emerging problems. Being able to change program direction quickly is a major characteristic of successful adult education organizations.

Recognizing Serendipity

Serendipity is a good thing happening that wasn't planned. When serendipity occurs, we are surprised and pleased, but if we are like some administrative leaders, we are perplexed and sometimes confused. Our confusion mounts if we are of the school that says, "Plan the work, work the plan, and measure the extent to which we reach the plan's objectives." What should we do with unplanned outcomes? Recognize them and applaud them. Often the most important outcomes of educational activities are those that no one anticipated—planners, administrators, participants, or anyone else.

For example, a university outreach dean attends a national conference designed to examine emerging societal trends. The dean sits by a business owner who, during a break, begins to describe how her business is reorganizing. The dean brings home a whole new perspective on organizational change—a topic not even discussed at the conference.

A middle manager enrolls in a yearlong leadership training program. By the end of the four sessions, he knows for certain that he does not want to become a top-level administrator. He has learned a great deal about himself during the workshops, and he proceeds to plan his career in a different direction.

Serendipity occurred both times; unintended but extremely valuable learning resulted. I could cite many examples, ranging from acquiring resources to solving major organizational problems. Good things happen beyond our efforts and sometimes in spite of our efforts. We need to recognize that they happened and accept them gladly even though it may appear that we didn't contribute much to their happening.

Organizational Spirituality

Just as it is essential for individuals to recognize the importance of their own spiritual side, it is also essential for organizations to consider spirituality. At a recent leadership workshop, we discussed organizational spirit. We made two lists of characteristics, one for an organization full of spirit and the other for an organization devoid of it. In organizations devoid of spirit, people said they felt unconnected and alone, tired, exhausted, rejected, unappreciated, depressed, deflated, diffused, scattered, powerless, and marginalized. In organizations full of spirit, the descriptions included celebration, a sense of oneness, a feeling of being fully human and alive, a small glimpse of heaven, a peak experience, interacting and connecting with others, excitement, enthusiasm, feeling uplifted, and being a part of something bigger than oneself.

At another level, organizational spirit relates to the core of what an organization believes and values. I refer to this as an organization's sacred core—its essence after the organizational charts, policy books, and operational guidelines have been stripped away. The sacred core of an organization should be reflected in everything the organization says about itself (mission, vision, plans), and in everything it does (care for staff, relationship to participants and stakeholders, role of knowledge). What can leaders do to help contribute to organizational spirit? Here are some practical ideas:

- See everyone as human beings, not as numbers, positions or roles.
- Recognize and appreciate the uniqueness of each person— staff, program participants, advisory committee members.
- Allow people to share their spirit. This includes accepting people's emotions and stories about who they are.
- Make room for joy in the organization. If appropriate, organize a joy club. Ben and Jerry's Ice Cream Company in Vermont has such a club. The group organizes birthday parties, softball teams, spontaneous celebrations, recognitions, and a host of other activities designed to bring joy to Ben and Jerry's business environment.
- Encourage learning together as well as playing together.
- Keep people involved and informed about what the organization is doing.
- Make sharing power a reality.
- Assist with organizational change and renewal. Work toward applying the concepts of a learning organization (Senge, 1990).
- Take time to celebrate the small successes as well as the big ones.
- Encourage time for organizational reflection as well as individual reflection.

Organizational Development and Renewal

There was a time when administrative leaders paid little attention to organizational change. They saw their role as making the organization work, and except for periodic reshuffling of boxes and lines due to retirements or budget adjustments, little effort was made to tamper with the organization's structure. As a result of this attitude, many adult education organizational structures have changed very little since they were first set up. Today's leader, upon examining the organizational structure in which he or she works, may discover that a goal is to effect adjustments in the structure. Thus, an appropriate leadership outcome may be an organizational change. Many of the ideas for a new perspective on adult education require new organizational structures as well as new approaches to leadership, with attention to the assumptions and thinking of the emerging age.

The predominant organizational structure followed by most adult and continuing education organizations is a pyramid, usually based on a military model. As Drucker (1992) points out, "One hundred and twenty-five years ago, when larger enterprises first came into being, the only organizational structure they had to model themselves on was the army: hierarchial, command-and-control, line and staff" (p. 30).

The dean, director, president, chair, or other top administrative leader sits at the peak of the pyramid. Several boxes are lined up under the top box, and so on, each succeeding layer of boxes wider than its predecessor, with lines connecting them all.

It is a system that has withstood the test of the time; it has worked, often well. This approach to organizational structure is based on the following assumptions:

- Everyone in the organization is responsible to one other person, with the exception of the person at the pyramid's peak, who is responsible to a board, council, or similar group.
- People are supervised by the person to whom they report. The supervisor largely determines work assignments and is responsible for supervising to make certain that the work is completed.
- The supervisor is responsible not only for allocating the work to be done and supervising its completion but also for decid-

ing whether subordinates should receive salary increases and promotions.

- The work setting is generally competitive among individuals. Persons who outperform their peers are rewarded with greater salary increases and more frequent promotions.

- Group effort is often discouraged. It is difficult to assess an individual's performance when the person works in a group.

- The supervisor, alone or in cooperation with the person, decides what the person should learn to improve performance and often makes specific suggestions as to how the learning should be accomplished—attend a workshop, enroll in a course, and so on.

- Staff members do not communicate with persons in other organizational units without following the "line of command"—going up the organization through supervisors and then back down again until the appropriate person is reached. At each step, some level of permission is requested to speak with the person in the other unit.

- Staff members do not communicate outside the organization without having the communication flow through their supervisor. Depending on how sensitive the communication is deemed to be, several layers of supervisors may need to give permission for the communication to occur.

- The pyramidal approach, with various modifications and adjustments, fits all organizations, for-profit or non-profit.

There are exceptions to these assumptions in top-down organizations, but generally they hold true. An outcome for leadership for the emerging era of adult education is to question present organizational structures and offer alternatives. Concepts such as shared leadership and empowerment, interdisciplinary offerings, ability to respond quickly to individual and community needs, and developing an organizational spirit require nonpyramidal organizational structures.

Just as leadership for the emerging age varies with context, so will organizational structure. Some adult education organizations, after careful examination, may well continue to follow a pyramid or a modified pyramid structure. This will probably be true for many college and university extension units, human resource development departments, and other adult education units that are themselves embedded in a larger pyramidal organization. But some of these adult education organizations may be able to move toward an alternative form, even when the larger unit does not. Indeed, some adult education organizations, willing to examine and risk new structures, may provide the impetus for the larger organization to change.

Today's organizational development literature offers many alternative structures. Handy (1989) talks about a shamrock organization; Helgeson (1990) discusses a spiderweb approach; Drucker (1992) talks about the organization as an orchestra; Morgan (1986) offers an array of organizational structures; Kanter (1983) discusses segmented and integrated organizations; Block (1987) examines the politics of organizational change and talks about a "pancake structure"; Bolman and Deal (1991) describe approaches for reframing organizations; and Schein (1992) examines organizational culture. There are many other models and perspectives to consider. It is not the purpose of this book to examine alternative organizational structures in depth or to offer strategies for organizational development and renewal. But this effort is clearly a responsibility for many adult education leaders these days.

Some alternative organizational structures are beginning to emerge. Earlier I mentioned the cooperative extension organization that chose not to fill a middle-management district director position and to have the functions of the position carried out by a team of staff people. A continuing education department within a university operates without a departmental head but with the administrative functions shared by several staff members. A national continuing education organization recently reorganized as follows: four senior managers handle the daily responsibilities of the headquarters office, formerly handled by the executive director. In the old organizational structure, information flow was up to the executive director, who made decisions based on the information he received. Now the management team meets weekly, with or without the executive director, and makes operational decisions. The information flow is across to other managers, and as a group they make an increasing number of decisions, as well as recommendations to the executive director.

One other feature of their new structure is a "quality service meeting" each Friday afternoon. The frontline staff, customer service, receptionist, sales, and bookkeeping people get together with one or more of the managers to discuss the week's events from the frontline staff perspective. The idea is to reverse the information flow so that it moves up as well as down. Frontline staff report on what customers are telling them, what trends they see, where the action is, the kinds of complaints received, what people like, and so on. Problems that surface are viewed as system problems, not individual problems, and the group works on the solutions. Many side benefits have resulted from these meetings, which offer opportunities to share frustrations, to ask for support, and to lighten the load through humor.

The challenge for leaders is to examine the context of their organization, including its vision, mission, and a host of other factors, and then develop a structure that will help the organization accomplish its purposes.

In many organizations this task is enormous. Tom Peters (1987) writes, "We are strangled by bloated staffs made up of carping experts and filling too many layers on the organization chart. . . .

It is now all too apparent that our overly centralized, overlayered organizations are dysfunctional" (pp. 355–358).

Individual change and learning is a given for all people, so it is also a given for all organizations. Thus, organizational change is clearly an expected outcome of leadership for the emerging age.

In the next chapter we begin looking at approaches to leadership, including a discussion of power and issues of gender and leadership.

Chapter Eight

Leading in New Ways

In developing a personal philosophy of leadership, the third component we must consider is leadership approaches. Once again, we begin by examining the context in which we work, to understand which leadership approaches have worked in the past and which are most comfortable for us. But we do not stop with this analysis. We must also focus on leadership approaches that are consistent with the emerging age.

Metaphors are useful in describing leadership approaches. Some people describe the process of leadership as a well-oiled, smooth-functioning machine, a football team, or a military battle. These metaphors mostly come from an old way of thinking about leadership and do not represent well the new perspective on adult education leadership.

Leadership metaphors for the new perspective on adult education leadership include the dance, the theater, or even the circus. The dance refers to working sometimes with partners but sometimes alone, trying to figure out the steps when the music is unfamiliar, staying off your partner's toes on a crowded dance floor, changing your step when the music changes, and so on. Leadership approaches are in many ways like a dance that lets us move around the floor, ideally with some grace and elegance, and at the same time have some fun.

The metaphor of the theater provides a different set of descriptors. Leadership often involves changing scenes with changing actors. Sometimes it is difficult to determine who has the lead;

indeed, in some plays the lead may change from scene to scene. People who are offstage—people the audience never sees—are essential to a successful production. The scriptwriter is a fundamental contributor to the entire process, even if a thousand miles away or long dead.

The circus is a fun metaphor for describing leadership approaches. In the circus, many things are going on at the same time, often seeming chaotic to the observer and sometimes to the participants as well. People have specialty roles: some know how to train animals; some swing from trapeze bars; some play in the band. Clowns lighten up the show, cover for errors and unforeseen occurrences, and provide a counterpoint to the serious business of trapeze artists flying through the air without a net. These metaphors and others help us adapt thinking about leadership approaches to the requirements of the emerging age.

The literature contains many references to leadership approaches. Some, such as being inspiring or using power, are not new. Other approaches we will discuss are less prominent in the literature. Because stormy-weather conditions, with unpredictable change, inspire leaders to develop approaches that no one has yet become aware of, the following discussion of leadership approaches is necessarily incomplete.

Approaches for Using Power

Power is the word most closely allied with leadership. Mention "leader," and people immediately think of someone in power. Power is also often associated with negative outcomes. We have many examples: Stalin was a leader with great power; so were Hitler and a host of other tyrannical political leaders. Power is too often seen as exploitative and manipulative, with a few people gaining and many losing. Power has long been associated with force: who has the largest army or the most deadly missiles. Brute power is easily understood.

For some people, power is determined by association. Who you know is a source of power; so is who your parents are. The kid in school whose father was president of the bank had power (or at least he thought he did). And "name droppers" hope not only that they will impress you but that they will have more power in your eyes.

Those of us in academia know about power through symbols; so does the rest of society. Few physicians omit "M.D." behind their names; even some Ph.D.'s have adopted the habit. And our society is obsessed with titles, in academia and everywhere else—assistant to the associate vice president, executive secretary, executive associate dean, executive head, associate executive head. With a title comes power, or so many people believe.

Power by sanction is another power source. Police officers, the military, and security guards have power by virtue of sanction.

And of course we must include power by position. Deans, departmental chairs, and unit heads have power—but until you sit in one of these positions, you can't know how fleeting their power can be. Power is too seldom seen in a positive light, as something that can engender good, create opportunities, and benefit many. James Burns (1978) writes, "Our main hope for disenthralling ourselves from our overemphasis on power lies . . . in seeing that the most powerful influences consist of deeply human relationships in which two or more persons *engage* with one another . . . [in] persuasion, exchange, elevation, and transformation. . . . We must see power—and leadership—as not things but as *relationships*" (p. 11).

Seeing power as a collection of relationships and not a thing is a key to leadership for the emerging age. A question I often ask participants in my leadership workshops is whether power is finite or infinite—whether there is a certain quantity of power in a situation or if it has the potential to endlessly increase. The root of this argument is in whether one sees power as a measurable entity or as a series of relationships that has the potential for becoming ever wider and deeper.

I am always surprised at the number of people, many of them middle managers and upper-level administrators in continuing education agencies, who reply that power is limited and must be protected. I clearly recall a woman who argued the point emphatically. "If I am to continue as a leader in my organization," she said, looking me straight in the eye, "I must protect every little bit of power I have."

As the workshop continued, she began to see another way of thinking about power. For people who have grown up with the idea of power as strength, control, and top-down direction, rethinking the definition of power is a struggle. Yet rethinking the definition of power and how it is applied is key to defining the essence of leadership for the emerging age. One premise of this approach to leadership is that power is shared, not hoarded; that power is given away, freely and often; that power is made available to everyone in the organization.

A paradox of leadership for the emerging age is that the more power the leader gives away, the more power the leader has. But it is a different kind of power. It is the power of relationships; it is the power of people relating to other people. It is the power of shared decisions, of persuasion, of discussion, of transformation.

To understand the roots of power in leadership situations, it is helpful to examine uses of power. In today's adult education organizations, it is relatively easy to find examples of each of these.

Power Through Fear

Stephen Covey (1991) describes power through fear this way: "Followers follow out of fear—they are afraid of what might happen to them if they don't do what they are asked to do. . . . The leader . . . has created a fear in the followers that either something bad is going to happen to them or something good will be taken away from them if they do not comply" (pp. 101–102).

When I was in the military, I encountered a captain who led by fear. He was a huge man with a strong, powerful voice and a vocabulary spiced with cusswords. I was assigned, briefly, to a harbor company, and our task was to load and unload ships. Stevedoring had never been high on my list of occupational objectives, yet there I was, in Virginia, deep in the hold of a ship under the watchful eye of Captain X, who showered on us a constant stream of invective. We all did what had to be done, although to a person we hated the task and our taskmaster.

In recent times I have encountered in adult education units more leaders than I thought existed who led by fear. I've found them in small units and large, in all parts of the country. Staff people resent them and complain to me about them. (I often arrive as a consultant to help a unit with a particular problem or to do an external evaluation of a department, school, or college, and end up learning far more about the organization than I had intended.)

Unfortunately, those who lead by fear are seldom aware of alternative approaches to leading, or if they are, they are too insecure to try a different leadership approach. They are tied to the concept of finite power, and they want all of it.

Power Through Transaction

Transaction is a popular leadership approach, well accepted in many organizations and often quite effective. It involves an exchange between leader and followers. As long as followers believe that they are being treated fairly, receiving adequate salaries and other benefits, they will continue to perform. As Covey (1991) points out, "It is being increasingly acknowledged that relationships based on utility power often lead to individualism rather than teamwork and group effectiveness, as each individual is reinforced or paying attention to [a personal] perspective and desires" (pp. 103–104).

The idea of individual stardom has long been the cornerstone of college and university administrations—reward the stars with higher salaries and greater perks. That is why this approach to leadership and power remains common in college and university extension and continuing education units.

A variation of power through transaction is the leader who knowingly or unknowingly plays a paternalistic role. Not only are services exchanged for salary and benefits, but the paternalistic leader looks after persons for whom he or she is responsible like the parent of a large family. There is genuine concern for relatives who are ill and other staff misfortunes and problems. But as in any family, everyone wants to be on the head of the household's "good side." Being on the good side of the paternalistic leader means producing beyond minimal expectation.

In my early years as a university extension agent, several of my immediate supervisors were paternalistic leaders. The situations were not entirely negative or even unpleasant. I knew what I was supposed to do, I did it, and I was rewarded accordingly. Missing was my involvement in deciding what I would do and how I would do it. My paternalistic supervisor, with good intentions because he didn't want me to fail, guided me in everything I did. It was only later, when I had moved on to another position, that I realized how confining and stifling working in such a situation can be, even though I knew exactly what was expected of me and I was rewarded well.

Power Through Charisma

I have known a few charismatic leaders and have worked for one who had great power by virtue of who he was, how he talked, how he walked, the very presence he commanded when he walked into a room. At semiannual staff meetings our director spoke to us. He had a commanding voice and a vast vocabulary, and he often quoted poetry. The 350 staff members sat spellbound as our director outlined where we were and where we were headed. He always asked for questions or comments at the end of his presentation. There were never any. Instead, he received standing ovations.

The true charismatic leader is one who trusts and honors fellow staff people as well as everyone who is in any way involved with a program, from the support staff to program participants. Charismatic leaders have vision, cleave to deeply held values, and know what they believe.

People follow such leaders out of sincere admiration, not because they want something in return. Charismatic leaders are often extremely important for newly formed organizations that are feeling their way and attempting to carve out their programming niche. Charismatic leaders have the ability to excite people about an organization and to assist them in developing deep commitments to an organization's mission.

On the downside, in some situations an organization and its staff become so dependent on a charismatic leader that when the leader leaves, chaos ensues. Another leader just like the one who left is sought and, of course, cannot be found.

A charismatic leader who makes all the important decisions for an organization can cause grave difficulty when an inappropriate decision is made. A loyal staff will follow an organization into oblivion in these circumstances.

Power Through Empowerment

The process of empowering, from the administrative leader's perspective, is both giving power (sharing power) and acknowledging the power that already exists in people. Empowering includes recognizing the broad and widely diverse kinds of power that reside in different cultures, ethnic groups, and geographic locations. It means considering power broadly, beyond a simple, single definition.

Leaders do not fully honor the concept of empowerment merely by giving power to others. By being in charge of power to be given away, they continue to control the power in the organization. Accepting the power that already exists in the diversity of people in an organization goes several steps beyond the sharing of power.

For the administrative leader, empowering means encouraging people to act on their own and then take responsibility for their actions. Lest this sound like anarchy, let me quickly say that empowerment does not mean that individuals go off and do whatever they please, irrespective of what others in the organization are doing. It means that individuals work together to decide on organization vision and mission and are then allowed to carry out various aspects of the mission as appropriate to their positions in the organization.

Within the general framework of a task, people decide what exactly they must do and how they will do it. Along with empowerment comes accountability: people have the right to act but must be accountable for their actions. Let me use a simple example. In a national leadership development program that I directed, the staff and I decided to offer a series of workshops. Earlier we had obtained considerable information about leadership needs and other leadership programs from a national advisory committee. One staffer's responsibility included making local arrangements. We had agreed that one workshop with a focus on diversity would include home visits with families in central Alabama. The staffer contacted people in Alabama to assist her, and soon all the arrangements were made. I was not involved in any way in the selection process, as I might have been. She knew what we were trying to accomplish with the home visits and the workshop generally and carried out the task beautifully.

For some leaders, the concept of empowerment does not move beyond the theoretical. They mouth the words but do little to carry out the actions. For many leaders, a personal transformation is necessary before empowering others can take place. Empowerment means a new way of thinking about power—power as infinite rather than finite, power as a set of relationships rather than as a thing.

Power and Leaders for the Emerging Age

Earlier I talked about sources of power: through association, symbols, sanction, and position. A major source of power for a leader comes from within: a clear personal credo and an understanding of fundamental beliefs and values that provide a compass for the person's life (see Chapter Four). The leader's power also comes from relationships and sharing, from recognizing and honoring power in others. Power is a positive force for stimulating and adapting to change. Power is in people, not in symbols, positions, or associations.

Following are a few additional approaches to leading.

Inspiring

Leaders, through example, inspire the people with whom they work. During times of turmoil, budget troubles, organizational change, and upheaval, inspiration is often in short supply. Inspiring means encouraging, supporting, and enlivening.

Renewing

Leaders are lifelong learners and encourage others to become the same. Walter Anderson (1990) makes the necessity of a lifetime of learning abundantly clear. "We come to accept the centrality of learning to the life of every individual, to every society, and to the species as a whole" (p. 258). Anderson also argues that a different kind of learning is necessary. "The kind of learning that becomes a necessity for survival in the postmodern age—the discovery kind of learning—is a bit different. It is not so much the constant filling in of a picture as an ongoing process of reality-construction in which it frequently becomes necessary to step out of the picture, and sometimes to drop the old picture entirely" (p. 258).

Peter Senge (1990) says, "Real learning gets to the heart of what it means to be human. Through learning we re-create ourselves. Through learning we do something we never were able to do. Through learning we extend our capacity to create, to be part of the generative process of life" (p.14).

Both Senge (1990) and Anderson (1990) talk about learning as transformation (see Chapter Eleven), a process whereby old ideas are set aside and replaced with entirely new ways of thinking. Such is the learning required of leaders as they face stormy-weather conditions with lightning-fast change that is often unpredicted. As outlined in Chapter Ten, leaders for the emerging age have a learning map that is never completed. They are always learning deliberately, as well as taking advantage of learning situations that occur at unplanned times.

I vividly recall a situation that arose when I first became a departmental chair. It involved a budget problem. I thought I had the problem solved until a dean overruled my decision and the whole thing came apart. I was angry and upset. After cooling off, I decided I would learn as much as I could about budget policies, which frankly hadn't interested me much before that incident. I talked with other departmental chairs who had been in similar situations. I studied the written rules and procedures. I learned a great deal from a situation that initially was fraught with emotion, bad feelings, and negativism. The budget was not restored, but I knew how I would handle budget situations differently in the future.

Leaders learn to reflect on their actions; they prize and seek out moments of solitude when they have time to confront themselves, challenge their challenges, and face their demons. Leaders accomplish what Senge (1990) calls personal mastery: "Personal mastery goes beyond competence and skills, though it is grounded in competence and skills. It goes beyond spiritual unfolding or opening, although it requires spiritual growth. It means approaching one's life as a creative work, living life from a creative as opposed to reactive viewpoint" (p. 141).

Too often, top-level administrators believe that they are too busy being administrators to step back, assess what they are doing, and work at self-renewal. Recently, at a workshop I conducted for about sixty-five adult education middle managers, I asked how many of the group had read a book in the past month. Three hands went up. "We've no time to read beyond the pile of memos, reports, and letters that pile up on our desks each day," several of them told me. Leaders for the emerging age read books of all kinds, from those directly related to their work to far-reaching nonfiction and fictional works that give them a broader perspective on their lives, their organizations, and their work.

Of the three people whose hands went up, one woman mentioned that she averaged a couple of books a month on a variety of topics. She read fiction as well as nonfiction, and she kept up with the professional reading that was directly related to her job. Leaders find time in their busy schedules to participate in a host of self-renewal activities, from attending formal classes to travel to solitude and reflection to developing a hobby that is totally unrelated to their work.

Leaders are also constant supporters of renewal for the people with whom they work, at every level. Business and industry, I believe, are often considerably ahead of adult education organizations in this regard. A recent visit to British Columbia revealed that learning centers had been set up in a number of firms. An employee could stop by the center before work, during noon break, after work, and at other arranged times. A learning coordinator was on hand to help the employee become aware of available learning opportunities. Employees could check out video and audio tapes on a variety of topics, many of them unrelated to the company's activities (for instance, an employee could listen to tapes teaching foreign languages). The learning center also displayed computerized lists of credit and noncredit courses offered in the community that the employee could sign up for—with financial assistance provided by the firm.

Variations on this approach can be found in firms throughout North America and in other parts of the world. The irony is that

educational organizations often overlook the fact that their employees, too, must be encouraged and assisted with their self-renewal.
Too often the employees are responsible for paying their own
tuition when attending formal classes. Too often employees are
encouraged to attend only educational functions that are directly
related to their jobs, with no mention of the value of broader educational activities.

Teaching

A leader for the emerging age is a teacher, but not just a traditional
giver of information, although that is part of the role. The leader
as teacher is a counselor, a supporter, an encourager, a modeler, a
challenger, and a questioner. The leader as teacher helps people
learn how to work together in groups, support each other, and learn
from each other. In these situations, the leader becomes a manager
of learning, assisting the learning groups in finding resources and
carrying the results of learning from one group to other groups in
the organization. The leader respects indigenous knowledge,
embraces it, and passes it on to others. For the leader, knowledge
takes many forms. It comes from reflecting on experience, it comes
from experience of the past, it comes from research and scholarship, it comes from moments of solitude.

Covey (1991) makes it clear that there is a time to teach and
a time not to teach. He says the best times for teaching are when
people are not threatened and when the leader is not angry or frustrated. It is not a good time to teach when people are in immediate need of assistance or are emotionally low or under a great deal
of pressure. Teaching during such times, Covey says, is akin to "trying to teach a drowning man to swim" (p. 126).

In addition to teaching individuals, leaders for the emerging
age are teachers of their organizations. Just as individuals in an
organization, at all levels, must continue to learn throughout their
lifetimes, so must organizations continue to learn. Organizations of
course learn through individuals, but just because individuals are

learning does not mean that the organization is learning. The leader must be a student of organizational change and renewal and a teacher of it as well. As people change, grow, and develop, so must organizations change, grow, and develop, and one of the leader's responsibilities is to help it happen.

Vision Making

Increasingly, leaders must be vision makers. This does not mean that they by themselves create the vision for their organizations. Indeed not, for vision making for the emerging age is a shared process, just like power.

The process of vision making involves several phases: making everyone in the organization aware of the importance of a vision, leading the vision-making process, and encouraging an examination of vision from time to time as people and conditions change.

The administrative leader for the emerging age is committed to vision making, which means a shared process. Administrative leaders must continue to have vision, but they must develop the capacity to involve the entire organization in a process of shared vision making where everyone, from the administrative leader to the clerical worker, has a say in what the vision will be. Folded into this mix are participants in the various programs. This means, for tax-supported institutions, representatives of bodies that make funding decisions. It also means contributions from community leaders and others who have contact with the organization in one way or another (see Chapter Seven for a more detailed description of vision making).

Challenging

Leaders for the emerging age are challengers of ideas, structures, assumptions, and beliefs. Leaders challenge themselves and their decision making. They also challenge others inside and outside the organization. I recall a colleague who worked with me in a staff and organizational development unit. Our challenge was to work with the continuing education organization of which we were a part, to develop long-range staff development plans and to examine organizational development issues.

More than once my colleague read my reports and recommendations and then covered the pages with comments and questions. Many times, after receiving her comments, I vowed never to share my work with her again. But after a day or so of moving past my anger and frustration, I discovered that her questions and comments were challenging me to produce something far better than I had. She often said to me and others, "When you think you've gone as far as you can with something, consider it a good beginning, and then go further."

Such challenging is not mean-spirited, nor is it done in an arrogant or demeaning way. The leader simply does not accept any aspect of the organization, including its structure, without careful scrutiny. This does not mean that the leader is opposed to change, new ideas, and new directions; far from it. In some instances a new idea is tried before it is carefully considered in every way. Such intensive careful consideration often kills off new ideas before they are ever tried.

Perhaps more appropriately, leaders challenge off-the-shelf approaches to programming or organizational change. Leaders challenge any elaborately developed approach to programming that is promoted as the "breakthrough approach that educators of the future will follow."

Leaders create an atmosphere within the organization in which people will learn to think and to consider the contexts of what they are doing and then make decisions accordingly rather than blindly accepting other people's ideas about why or how things should be done. Being a challenger contributes to taking charge of one's own leadership, no matter where the person happens to be within an organization.

Using Humor

In a society that seems to be increasingly high pressured and focused on results, humor is sometimes sacrificed in the haste to get things done as efficiently as possible. Rather than using up valuable time and seemingly diverting attention from the task at hand, humor serves many valuable purposes. First, and most fundamental, humor is a natural, human characteristic. We feel good when we laugh. We relax. Humor can surprise us; it can teach as well. An appropriate humorous story can make a point far more effectively than a dreary rundown of facts or details.

With humor we can be more accepting of our own mistakes by laughing when we goof. It demonstrates that we are human and that we don't take ourselves overly seriously. Humor can also help cement relationships with our co-workers. It can calm emotions and reduce tensions when there are honest differences of opinion among decision makers. But we must be cautious in using humor as well. Humor is never used to demean a person or a group. To poke fun at a person who disagrees with us is never appropriate, and it is always inappropriate to poke fun at ethnic, religious, or racial groups, physical appearance or handicaps, or other irrelevancies.

Some people use humor naturally; it is a part of their personality. Other people simply aren't very funny. Humor cannot be contrived. You can't say, "Now I must be funny." Humor used in this way may backfire.

Most of us, when we rediscover ourselves, uncover a humorous streak. It is a natural characteristic of most human beings. And it's fun to allow this humorous streak to come out in a good-natured way in our day-to-day activities.

Sometimes an administrative leader has to say, in effect, "It's OK to have some humor in this organization." That's a sad commentary on how serious some adult education organizations have become. Recently, a director of continuing education told me that one of his goals was to see more joy in his organization. I think that's a terrific goal.

Building Bridges

Leaders are often called on to build bridges between people and between ideas. In an increasingly diverse world, the challenge is to emphasize both-and rather than either-or. Leaders must bring together diverse perspectives and garner the best from these perspectives for the organization while at the same time fostering relationships among people that allow them to work together.

A resource development director in a large eastern-based firm is working to build bridges between his organization and the land grant university in his state. A small group of top-level administrators in the university's continuing education unit began talking with the firm's human resource development department about possible links between them. Early meetings have allowed the two groups to get acquainted with each other's programs and purposes. One challenge they discovered early is to understand the other's language and jargon. The first action step they decided on was to enroll a continuing education administrator in the firm's executive development program.

The premise behind the concept of bridge building is moving past the idea of judging the rightness and wrongness of people and ideas to an idea of accepting the best of an array of positions. (The concept of both-and rather than either-or is discussed further in Chapter Two.)

Tolerating and Even Encouraging Discomfort

Administrative leadership has always had its moments of discomfort. The amount of discomfort does not decrease as we move into the emerging age; indeed, it may well increase. The key for the administrative leader now and in the future is to learn to tolerate the discomfort. One way to do that is to recast discomfort as a positive aspect of leading. And to take the idea a step further, leaders may at times find it useful to encourage a little discomfort in their organizations. A little discomfort creates awareness and challenges complacency, which is the curse of many adult education organizations.

The key is to balance the comfort and discomfort levels within an organization. Too much discomfort leads to an assortment of problems, such as low morale and decreased productivity. But too little discomfort can lead to the same results. The challenge is finding the proper balance.

Encouraging Artistry

Too often in recent years, the leadership literature has emphasized a technical, scientific approach to leading. Peter Vaill (1989) and Max De Pree (1989) have both argued that artful elements of leading must also be considered. The technical approach to leading, with its emphasis on facts, analysis, and rationality, is not enough for sound leadership decision making (see Chapter Four). De Pree (1989), for instance writes, "Leadership is an art, something to be learned over time, not simply by reading books. Leadership is more tribal than scientific, more a weaving of relationships than an amassing of information, and, in that sense, I don't know how to pin it down in every detail" (p. 3).

A key to understanding the art of leadership is to accept that it cannot be understood, certainly not in the same way as scientific ideas about leadership can be understood. The artful dimensions of leadership are *felt*; they are embedded in the leader's spirit rather than in the person's intellect.

An artful approach to leadership takes the leader deeply into situations, allowing understanding at levels that go well beyond scientific understanding. Vaill (1989) says, "The artist is after . . . 'something more,' determined to find coherence and meaning embedded more subtly and deeply in experience than the rest of us see. The artist is after a theme, a dimension, an aspect of existence that no one else seems to see in quite the same way" (p. 40). The challenge for leaders in the emerging age is to understand and apply the scientific knowledge about leadership and at the same time work at following an artful approach to leading.

Gender and Leadership Approaches

A question that has arisen in recent years, particularly since women have become prominent in the work force, is, do women and men lead differently? There is some evidence that the answer is yes, at least in certain areas.

Sally Helgeson (1990) studied in depth four women executives, representing one nonprofit and three for-profit organizations. She also examined recent research on the topic of women's leadership styles. From her work she concluded that women attend to the process of leadership more than the bottom line; they are concerned with how their actions will affect other people; they are interested in the broader needs of the community; they appreciate diversity; and they are impatient with "rituals and symbols that divide people who work together and so reinforce hierarchies" (pp. xx–xxi).

Carolyn Desjardins and Carol Brown (1991) conducted a study of seventy-two community college presidents and discovered several similarities but important differences based on gender. In such categories as political awareness and information gathering, no gender differences existed. But, they reported, "women excelled in presence (projecting enthusiasm and/or strength), optimism, initiative, decisiveness, persuasiveness, and interest in developing people. Men excelled in self-esteem, self-confidence, enjoying a challenge, self-control, involvement in change, and commitment to community service" (p. 19).

In a survey sponsored by the International Women's Forum, an organization of women leaders in diverse professions from around the world, Judy B. Rosener (1990) discovered that men "view job performance as a series of transactions with subordinates— exchanging reward for services rendered or punishment for inadequate performance. The men are also more likely to use power that comes from their organizational position and formal authority." By contrast, women were more likely to "transform their own self-interest into the interest of the group through concern for a broader goal" (p. 120). Women in the study said they gained their power from such sources as personal contacts, charisma, and interpersonal skills.

Rosener went on to interview several women in the study. From the interviews she concluded that women leaders encouraged participation and the sharing of power and information. She also concluded that these women leaders went well beyond the usual definitions of participation. A preponderance of these women leaders' efforts "were attempts to enhance other people's sense of self-worth and to energize followers. In general, these leaders believe that people perform best when they feel good about themselves and their work, and they try to create situations that contribute to that feeling" (p. 120).

Helen Astin and Carole Leland (1991), in a study of women leaders in education, concluded that women viewed leadership as collective action, requiring passionate commitment and consistent performance. A particularly interesting result of this study was the women's commitment to social justice and change. "Their passion comes in part from direct personal experiences: experiencing or witnessing discrimination. Their values stem from their roots: grandparents, parents, or other relatives who also cared passionately about social justice" (pp. 157–158).

There was a time when women were encouraged to think and behave like men if they were to become successful leaders. Helgeson (1990) quotes writers who said that women needed to "indoctrinate themselves in the military mind-set . . . and study the underlying dynamic of games such as football" (p. xvii). The assumption was that most organizations were organized similar to the military, with a top-down, pyramidal structure, and the leadership strategies used were in large measure based on sports such as football.

But today many leadership approaches that some claim come naturally to women—leading from the heart, not merely the mind; concern for the development of others; sharing of leadership; questioning of "military-style" organizations; and so on—are essential for leadership in the emerging age.

Helgeson (1990) concludes: "Pressed by global competition and a fast-changing technology characterized by flexibility and innovation, companies are casting aside old cultural values, trimming the pyramid, and rooting out cumbersome bureaucratic structure. . . . The old chain-of-command hierarchy, with its unspoken rules and codes, is too lumbering and muscle-bound for today's economy" (pp. xviii, xix). Much of what Helgeson says about companies can of course be said about adult education organizations, which in many respects followed the organizational patterns and leadership strategies of the business world.

Different Perspectives on Leading

As leaders for the emerging age become more and more comfortable with the pressures and challenges of rapidly changing and often chaotic leadership situations, several other perspectives guide them.

1. *Letting things happen.* This sounds like a nonapproach to leadership and certainly a contradiction of people who believe that leaders must always be in charge, must always make a difference, and an assortment of other things that I call "false truisms."

The laissez-faire approach to leadership, long discounted as a nonleadership approach, may have had more validity than the leadership researchers of the day would acknowledge. In laissez-faire leadership, the leader got out of the way and let things unfold in a natural way, without any leader intervention.

Benjamin Hoff (1982) writes, "If you are in tune with the way things work, then they work the way they need to, no matter what you may think about it at the time. Later on, you can look back and say, 'Oh, now I understand. That had to happen so that *those* could happen, and those had to happen in order for *this* to happen. . . .' Then you realize that even if you'd tried to make it all turn out perfectly, you couldn't have done better, and if you'd *really* tried, you would have made a mess of the whole thing" (p. 80). Sometimes leaders work too hard and push too much to make something happen. Sometimes stepping back for a time, relaxing, and backing off is a better strategy. A wise leader is one who knows when to push and when to sit on the bench.

2. *Thinking less and caring more.* Those of us who work in adult education, at every level, have learned to become thoughtful. We pride ourselves on our ability to "think things out." Sometimes we become overly dependent on our heads and fail to listen to our hearts. Leadership means thinking, but it also means caring. And caring comes from the heart. From time to time we must learn to switch off that wonderful brain of ours and ask ourselves what our hearts have to say.

Someone recently asked me, "How do I know when to let my heart take over in making a decision?" It isn't so much that we let our heart rule our decision making as it is to keep our heart turned on so that we can hear what it has to say along with what our brains are telling us. There are no criteria to follow, no guidelines that tell us here is where we should pay attention to our heart. As whole beings with minds and hearts, the challenge is to listen to both as we make decisions.

3. *Leading as we are.* In Chapters Four and Five, I discussed approaches for finding out who you are and how this knowledge can help you as a leader. Leading as we are means finding our inner nature and allowing it to guide us. As Hoff (1982) points out, "Inner nature, when relied on, cannot be fooled. But many people do not look at it or listen to it, and consequently do not understand themselves very much. Having little understanding of themselves, they have little respect for themselves, and are therefore easily influenced by others" (p. 57). The purpose for developing a personal philosophy of leadership is to give us a foundation for leading so that we can lead authentically, from the depths of who we are.

These are a few ideas about approaches to leadership. Leaders for the emerging age of adult education may find some of these useful, others less so. More important, leaders will develop their own approaches consistent with who they are and the requirements of their contexts. Many of their approaches will thus be unique.

The final component of a personal philosophy of leadership is an understanding of educational perspectives, the topic of the next chapter.

Chapter Nine

Developing New Educational Perspectives

Developing a personal philosophy of leadership requires that we examine ideas about leaders and their qualities and characteristics, outcomes of leadership, and leadership approaches. The emerging age challenges us to look at these components of leadership in new ways. Adult education leaders must also examine how the emerging age influences educational approaches taken by learners and teachers. In adult education organizations, administrative leaders must often assume the role of educational leader along with all of their other responsibilities. Invariably, a large number of the staff work part time and have little experience with approaches to teaching, understanding adults as learners, and the like. Thus administrative leaders become responsible for how their organizations conduct educational programs. The challenge, in these changing times, is to make sure that the educational approaches used are consistent with the requirements of the emerging age.

To assume the role of educational leader in some instances requires leaders to rethink how they themselves view various aspects of education. For example, old approaches to education have been based on a linear, hierarchical model with ties to the assumptions of the industrial age. Writers such as Eisner (1985) talk about present-day education as a "factory view," "an assembly-line conception of teaching and learning" with an interest in "the creation of measurable products, in the specification of criteria against which products can be judged, . . . in the talk about quality assurance and quality control," and the measurement of educational outcomes (p. 263).

Other assumptions of the industrial age of education include "a belief that everything can be known, codified, predicted and controlled through objective scientific examination, a perspective where there are always winners and losers, in which growth, efficiency and specialization are the highest good, and science and technology can solve all problems" (Crauthers, 1991, p. 55).

In the emerging age, education's foundation is "based on the idea that nature and humans are one, that wholes are more than the sum of their parts, that objectivity is neither necessary nor achievable, that study can reveal patterns but not certainties, and that the control of nature by humans for their own individual purposes must be replaced by a reverence for all things and their interconnectedness if life on this planet is to survive" (Crauthers, 1991, pp. 55–56).

In the emerging age, almost every facet of teaching and learning is questioned. Ideas to be questioned include the premise, still held by many, that learning is the accumulation of information, that information should be organized by disciplines, and that a primary reason for learning is the accumulation of credentials. Another assumption questioned is that education ought to be based on learner needs. Some learning should be based on learner needs, but certainly not all. As Drucker (1992) notes, "Learners need to know their strengths in order to find out where to improve. What bad habits inhibit these strengths? In what areas has the Good Lord simply not provided any ability at all? Most schools and most education are problem-focused; they concentrate on correcting weakness. Up to a point, that is necessary. Every student needs the basic skills. But world-beating performance, like learning, is built on strengths. When it is so organized, learning is astonishingly rapid, for the simple reason that it has focus" (p. 349). Other assumptions to be questioned include that only persons with the proper credentials can become teachers and that only those who are qualified to learn (as determined by the institution, agency, or organization) will have the opportunity to learn.

In the emerging age, everyone teaches at one time or another. An educator may be called a teacher, a tutor, a learning broker, a facilitator, a consultant, or a learning manager who points the way and then stands aside. Everyone is also a learner. Learning opportunities include courses, workshops, seminars, self-study opportunities, and learning at a distance. Subject matter is disciplinary, interdisciplinary, extradisciplinary, personal, and informal.

Many adult educators are aware of the kind of education that is becoming a part of the emerging age, for they have long been practicing education with these new assumptions in mind. But many other adult educators, especially those associated with formal schooling, teach at colleges, universities, and technical schools where the assumptions of the industrial age continue to undergird most educational programs.

As we move into this new age for adult education, the best research and practices of the past and present are brought forward. Much current research, scholarship, and experience in education has application in the emerging age; much does not. Needed are new approaches not yet researched or in some instances not yet even thought about.

Overview of Adult Education in the Emerging Age

In the emerging age, education and all of its manifestations— teachers and teaching, learners and learning, subject matter, purposes—are constantly examined at the deepest levels. The mind-set for all educators at every level is to improve the process and to keep it always relevant to the times and the context where it is being applied. This is not a new idea, of course. Educators of conscience have constantly sought such improvement over the years. But in the past many educators became comfortable with strategies and doctrine that they believed worked well, and they have stuck to them. Some of these educators have resisted critically examining what they do, why they do it, and who might benefit or be harmed by their efforts.

These are the educators that Giroux (1992) and Greene (1978) refer to as technicians and clerks who do their work unquestioningly and are subservient to others or to situations that have long remained the same. Greene, referring to teachers, writes, "If they undergo a purely technical training or a simplified 'competency based' approach, they are likely to see themselves as mere transmission belts—or clerks. The question of the freedom of those they try to teach, the question of their students' endangered selves; these recede before a tide of demands for 'basics,' 'discipline,' and preparation for the 'world of work.' Teachers (artlessly, wearily) become accomplices in mystification. They have neither the time, nor energy, nor inclination to urge their students to critical reflection; they, themselves, have suppressed the questions and avoided backward looks" (p. 38).

A second important focus for education in the emerging age is the interplay between learning for the individual and learning for the collective (community, societal, and organizational learning). No longer does learning relate solely to individuals and their problems and needs. Learning also focuses on organizations, communities, and the larger society. Educators are becoming skilled at both individual learning, with a focus on the person, and learning with an eye toward renewing organizations (sometimes referred to as organizational learning). Educators are becoming knowledgeable about the relationship of the two—how organizational learning influences the individual and how individual learning can influence the collective.

A third consideration is to relate various aspects of education: education occurring in educational establishments such as schools, colleges, and universities; education for youngsters and for adults; education for work and for leisure pursuits; education as a nonprofit activity and education for profit; and education designed and carried out by the learner (self-directed learning). No longer does it make sense to examine education and its purposes, strategies, and future directions without some attempt at examining it in a larger context. To be sure, certain aspects must be examined independently of others, but every examination is conducted with an eye to the totality. In the emerging age, it does not make sense to research and discuss aspects of adult education without attending to elementary, secondary, and higher education, nonprofit and for-profit activity, and education taking place outside of educational institutions.

Views About Learners

I was talking with a high-level university administrator recently about her institution's view of its students. She was very candid. She said, "We develop the best and process the rest." No matter how old the learners we are talking about, the emerging age requires more than developing a few and processing the many.

Much research in adult education until quite recently has focused on the generic adult learner. Some work has been done on age differences and life circumstances for learning (Apps, 1981, 1982; Aslanian and Bricknell, 1980; Cross, 1981; Hudson, 1991; Knox, 1977, 1986; Merriam and Caffarella, 1991; and Wlodkowski, 1993, among others). But even this research has largely focused on white middle-class people and how they learn. The emerging age requires that learner differences be examined more carefully than they have ever been in the past. Research by Belenky and others (1986), Gilligan (1982), and Estes (1992) reveals that women learn differently from men. Some recent work suggests that Native American cultural background influences how Native Americans learn (Dawson, 1992). Cultural histories also influence how African-Americans, Asian-Americans, Hispanics, and other cultural groups learn. In addition to culture and ethnicity, learning is also influenced by socioeconomic circumstance, previous learning experiences, nutrition, exposure to certain chemicals as children, and a host of other factors. Adult education must focus more on the context for learning, realizing that each context—the learner's history, the learner's current situation, and the larger societal situation—must be considered when developing educational opportunities.

Learners have the ability to take charge of their own learning and the responsibility to do so. An assumption of many educational systems, from preschool through graduate education and beyond, is that some outsider knows best what a person should learn. Increasingly, adults do not wait for others to tell them what, why, when, or how to learn. A silent rebellion against traditional courses and classes with inflexible times and traditional instruction is occurring as people grow more comfortable with their learning independence.

This newfound independence is expressed in the words *pace*, *place*, and *time*. Learners want something to say about how fast or how slowly they wish to learn (pace), where they learn (place)—they may prefer their living room over a classroom—and when they learn (time)—early morning, late afternoon, evenings or weekends.

Many learners in the emerging age become critical learners. With the flood of information available, learners are challenged to become competent evaluators of information. This means learning how to discern accurate from inaccurate information and relevant from irrelevant information. Information nowadays comes in attractive, appealing packages as information salespeople ply their trade. Learners must learn to untie the ribbon, peel back the wrapper, and examine what is inside. Some useful questions are: How do you know this? What are your sources? How does this information fit me and my situation? The fact that the information source is not a person or is not present should not prevent asking the questions or seeking the answers.

Taking charge of one's learning also means becoming aware of the blinders that prevent people from looking in the corners and closets where the information that may be most valuable to them is hidden. Learners' personal histories not only influence who they are and what they believe and value but also influence how and what they perceive. Recognizing that everyone has blinders is the first step toward removing them and letting in a broader range and depth of information (see Chapter Eleven).

Finally, taking charge of one's learning means not being overly concerned about credits, credentials, certificates, and diplomas. In today's society, pieces of paper attesting to learning accomplishments are important. But some of the most important learning results from situations where no credential exists. Examples include learning to be a grandfather, learning to appreciate a sunset on a cold winter day in the deafening quiet of a snow-covered landscape, discovering a new sense of life's meaning after the death of a loved one, or learning to face a new and baffling task with confidence and enthusiasm.

Learners in the emerging age are challenged by the future but not paralyzed by it. They are informed by the past but not tied to it. Learners walk the fine line between the comfort and familiarity of the past and the discomfort and unknowability of the future. Learners are thus often comfortable and uncomfortable at the same time—one of many paradoxes of the emerging age.

Learners coming into a new learning situation generally know far more than they believe they know. As learners begin taking charge of their own learning, they relax and often surprise themselves that they already know a great deal about a subject or situation they are trying to learn more about. Thus learning becomes not only adding new knowledge and perspectives but also uncovering and making sense out of what is already there.

In many areas, learners are not aware of what they do not know. Hence most learners appreciate challenges from instructors, from fellow learners, and from educational materials, be they books, video or audio tapes, or hands-on materials in the workplace. These challenges assist learners in becoming aware of what they don't know.

Adult Learning and Teaching

The emerging age requires people to go beyond accumulating information in the name of learning. People must learn how to examine information critically, apply it, relate it to previous learning, and be open to developing new perspectives about who they are and how they view their immediate and broader contexts as a result of their learning. Information is integral to learning, but there is much more to learning than merely accumulating it. (Note that I usually differentiate between knowledge and information. My knowledge becomes your information and your knowledge becomes my information until we both have wrestled with it, analyzed it, and attempted to apply it.)

An outdated assumption is that all learning outcomes can be measured. Many adult learning organizations have attempted to follow the lead of businesses that emphasize measuring outcomes for everything that employees do. Parker Palmer (1993a) reminds us of problems faced when education becomes obsessed with products and results:

> First of all, when we get obsessed with results, we take on smaller and smaller tasks, because they are the only ones [we] can get results with. Ultimately, when we get obsessed with results, we give up on educating students and simply train them to pass the test. We must fight that tendency in American culture that wants to measure everything by outcomes. Second, when results are the only measure of our work, we become very skilled at creating the illusion or the appearance of results rather than the real thing. I know why the lecture has been so popular as a method of teaching for so long. By filling the whole hour with lecture, you can make it *look* like education has happened whether it has or not (p. 5).

Some learning is certainly measurable, particularly learning that relates to knowledge gain and skill acquisition. But much learning, particularly higher-level learning that involves shifting one's way of thinking and developing new perspectives, is generally impossible to measure quantitatively. It is usually possible, though, to describe the changes that are occurring.

Change can be described in several ways, often through stories told by the learners. In a leadership development project that I have been involved with recently, we wrestled with the question, What are the participants gaining from this? Early on we dismissed simple paper-and-pencil inventories that attempt to measure knowledge gain because, we decided, the most important learning occurring in the program was probably at a level that couldn't be easily measured, if indeed it could be measured at all. So we asked participants to describe what they were doing in particular leadership situations. We also asked their colleagues to comment on changes they had seen in the participants. In the early stages of the program, after the participants had been involved for six months or so (the program was up to two years long for many participants), their colleagues provided us with extremely useful information. These associates were seeing changes in the participants—in how they related to people, in how they organized their time, in how they did their work—even before the participants themselves were aware of the changes. The colleagues' stories about the participants, describing the changes that were occurring, actually chronicled the learning that was taking place.

A second flaw with the idea that all learning can be measured is the assumption that someone other than the learner is always in a position to know best what the learner is learning. Again, in some instances this is true, particularly for learning in which certain standards must be met or in situations as just described where learners may not yet be completely aware of how they are changing. An example of a situation in which it is important to meet learning standards would be preparing people as emergency medical technicians. But other learning—the deeper, more personal learning through which someone's view of life or the world is altered—must be assessed by the learner, not by some outside observer. An observer can hold up a mirror or provide a perspective on how the learner is changing, but that is the best the outsider can do. To expect an outsider to assess a person's deeper changes in any kind of complete way is impossible.

In this emerging age, the metaphors for education are changing. The old metaphors of assembly lines and factories, of sports and the military, are declining. New metaphors of journeys, of dances, and of butterflies unfolding are emerging, along with a host of other metaphors not yet identified but implying cooperation, renewal of the spirit, and individual and organizational transformation.

Learners are recognized as whole people, each with a mind, a body, and a spirit, each element influencing the others. Just as the emerging medical literature underlines the mind as important in healing the body, so are the body and the spirit important in learning. (See Moyers, 1993, for an interesting discussion of the mind's role in healing the body.) Teachers recognize the importance of all three of these elements in their teaching and in their own development as teachers. To deny the power of the spirit and the body in learning, to concentrate solely on matters of the mind, is to fail to consider the uniqueness of the human condition. In the emerging age, learning includes feeding the spirit.

Parker Palmer (1993b) writes, "Authentic spirituality wants to open us to truth—whatever truth may be, wherever truth may take us. Such spirituality does not dictate where we must go, but trusts that any path walked with integrity will take us to a place of knowledge. Such a spirituality encourages us to welcome diversity and conflict, to tolerate ambiguity, and to embrace paradox" (p. xi).

Behind approaches to education that emphasize products and results and the measurement of outcomes is an assumption that teaching and learning can be treated as a technical activity consisting of prescribed approaches that lead to predictable outcomes, such as one would expect from a machine. Many educators have foolishly come to believe that teaching and learning can operate in such a machinelike fashion: feed in a certain amount of information, manipulate it, and predictable, measurable learning will occur.

What this approach to education misses is the joy of teaching and learning and their mystery and mystique. Missed are the unpredictable outcomes, learning that was not intended but that often proves more important than what was planned. Missed also is the exciting challenge for the teacher, who must face each situation as a new one, never quite sure what will happen or how but working with the knowledge that something will happen and that it will be good. Such teachers teach from the heart as well as from the mind. They teach with passion. They teach to refresh the spirit as well as challenge the mind. They teach with humor and with joy; they challenge and they encourage; they move rapidly with some learners, more slowly with others. These teachers in the emerging age realize that the shortest distance between two points is often not a straight line but a spiral, turning back on itself as learners pursue new ideas and challenges in relation to what they know, who they are, and where they have been.

Teachers in the emerging age know the subject they are teaching. They know how to organize it so that learners can grasp it easily, make meaning of it, and apply it to their own special context. Teachers know when to lecture, when to lead a discussion, or when merely to raise questions and let the process happen. They are comfortable using educational technology; in some instances they work with learners half a world away. Teachers learn to use technology not merely as an adjunct to current teaching approaches (bringing in an expert speaker via conference phone as part of a lecture) but as a unique approach to offering educational opportunities. Technology makes it possible to organize learning opportunities in fresh ways, using the potential of computer databases as information sources, allowing learners at remote locations to interact with each other, and encouraging learners to have more control over their learning.

Teachers do not fear putting themselves into their teaching, allowing their teaching to reflect who they are as human beings, encouraging their own voice as a person to show through. Some teachers will be certified and credentialed; others will not. The contributions of all teachers are accepted and applauded.

Learning for individuals occurs when they are alone and when they are with others. Too often we argue that certain people learn best when they are alone and others learn best in groups. In most instances, the issue is not either-or but both-and. In solitude, learners can reflect on what they are learning, often confronting themselves in the process and finding new meaning about who they are. In community, learners are confronted by others who can provide valuable comments on what the person is learning. To question, challenge, or disagree promotes learning at ever-deeper levels. When learning in community, learners can help change the community, and as they seek to change the community they are in turn changed themselves (see Chapter Ten).

Learning is always in relationship—with self, with others, and beyond. Learning in relationship means reading a novel and having the characters talk back, or becoming acquainted with a theory and saying, "Here's where I fit." Learning in relationship means hearing a piece of music or looking at a piece of art and feeling the effect of it. Learning in relationship also means relating what we are learning to our personal histories and contexts. Learning is never a static, objective, impersonal thing.

The outcomes of learning are many-faceted. Learners learn new skills, solve problems, connect with new knowledge, search for meaning in life, satisfy curiosity, seek to improve their communities, refresh their souls, and experience transformation whereby self and world are viewed in a dramatically different way.

For the teacher, teaching means moving from telling to sharing, from adding to a learner's store of information to integrating new information with old, from serving as an expert source of knowledge to becoming a questioning, sharing journey leader. Teachers must deplore learner passivity and encourage active involvement. Teachers increasingly become students of context, for all learning occurs in an often complicated, ambiguous context.

Learning includes developing personal and work-related skills but goes well beyond enhancing one's economic position. Learning includes developing critical-thinking skills, accumulating knowledge, revealing inner truth, finding meaning in life, discovering one's unique voice and perspective, learning for the joy of it, healing (memories of historical events, personal relationships, successes and failures), and transforming (evolving as one learns).

The process of learning includes clearing the mind. Clearing the mind involves, at one level, removing inner and outer barriers to learning. Inner barriers to learning include fear of taking charge of one's learning; fear of failing, succeeding, or changing; and fear of the struggle that learning often requires. All these fears become demons for some learners and prevent them from learning at the depth required in the emerging age.

Learners who have been told by outsiders what, how, and why to learn often fear the unknown when they take charge of their own learning. Some do not know how to proceed, and become paralyzed. Some require assistance in developing a learning plan. For some this is a difficult and challenging task, particularly if they continue to wrestle with such questions as, Will I learn the right things? and, Have I selected the right approaches for learning?

In the workshops I conduct that are offered in a series to the same participants, I encourage participants to develop their own learning plans (with assistance) covering what they want to learn during the year (see Chapter Ten). I offer several planned activities, including face-to-face workshops and suggested readings, but most of the yearlong program is planned by each participant. For many participants, developing an individual learning plan is one of the most difficult parts of the program, something most participants have never done before.

Along with the fear of taking charge of one's learning is an ongoing fear of failing. If I don't learn the *right* things I will not be promoted or will not succeed in my job. And the converse is also true: if I succeed in my learning, I will face a promotion with new responsibilities and new people, and my current way of doing things will be disrupted. Underneath this fear is, of course, a fear of change. Many people, though they may say otherwise, enjoy stability. Learning is often disruptive and involves change. And change, for many people, becomes a struggle, something they would prefer to avoid.

External barriers also prevent learning. External barriers include participating in education activities where the emphasis is on presenting information with little or no time for learner reflection, learning situations that are overly competitive, situations in which success is measured by an outsider, and "standardized" learning with little or no attention to the learner's context. Other barriers include lack of access to learning opportunities because they are too expensive, offered at inconvenient times or in inconvenient places, or presented in formats not suited to the learner.

Many credit programs, and some noncredit programs as well, insist on individuals' competing for grades. So much is possible in cooperative learning, yet when students cooperate, we call it cheating. As mentioned earlier, adult learners should have at least some responsibility in the assessment of their learning. Others can help them by providing standards and guidelines, but the learners should be actively involved in the process.

Beyond dealing with internal and external barriers for learning, clearing the mind means establishing boundaries for learning so that learners do not become overwhelmed. Establishing boundaries is an important dimension of taking charge of one's own learning, paying attention to the bigger picture, the totality of what is to be learned, but at the same time attempting to learn in reasonable bites. The concept of "small wins" might be applied here. The old saw about learning to walk before entering the Boston Marathon might be applied as well. Organizing one's learning in bite-size pieces can help prevent being intimidated by the vastness of the full picture.

Finally, clearing the mind means developing the capacity for hearing the whispers in one's life and in one's learning. Most of us, often out of necessity, must respond to the shouts—the demands placed on us, the problems we encounter, the challenges we face every day. But often we are so engrossed with the shouts that we fail to hear the whispers, the ideas that are not currently popular, the approaches that a few people are following but the majority dismiss out of hand, the ideas found in novels and poetry that seem at the moment to have no connection to one's life. It is often in the whispers that entirely new strategies for leading are born, entirely new approaches for organizing are found, and entirely new thinking about learning resides. The first step in developing the capacity for hearing the whispers is to take the attitude that the unusual today may be the mainstream tomorrow, that what seems strange today may someday be commonplace. To attend to the whispers, we must learn to see and not just look, feel and not just touch, listen and not just hear.

Learning and Life

In the emerging age, learning becomes an integral part of life, as it is for many people now. Much learning takes place as people live and face situations they haven't faced before. They increasingly become reflective learners. They experience, and as they experience, they learn. In some instances they have time to experience and then reflect on the experience and learn from it. In other situations they experience and learn simultaneously, as when there is no time to reflect on what has been learned. "Learning while doing" is not a new idea. Most of us have already done it, sometimes knowingly, sometimes not. For canoeists, paddling through white-water rapids is an example of experiencing and making immediate adjustments. The white-water canoeist paddles fiercely, reads the water, and changes paddling strategy immediately. Learning and action are mixed together.

Increasingly, all of us confront situations that are not anticipated. Many of these situations have never been experienced by anyone, and hence we cannot learn in advance any specific skills or perspectives that will assist us. All of us can benefit from developing the capacity to learn as we do and move beyond the long-standing premise that we learn in preparation for doing.

As part of a leadership development program, thirty adult education middle managers set out on a four-day canoe trip on the Missouri River. The purpose of the trip was to demonstrate and experience teamwork, understand oneself in new situations, and become acquainted with Native American cultural sites along the river. After canoeing during the day, the group spent the evenings tenting on the riverbank.

The trip planners had not reckoned on a severe thunderstorm that struck one night, dumping several inches of rain and tearing down several tents. In the dreary wet dawn of the following day, the trip leaders, with participant assistance, completely replanned the remainder of the trip. Group members spent time discussing what they had learned from the storm and how some of that learning was at least as important as the learning that had been planned.

In the emerging age, we prepare for some situations and, through learning, develop skills, competencies, and perspectives. But for many situations we cannot prepare in any detailed or systematic way. Our preparation includes such things as becoming comfortable with unusual, never-before-faced situations and accepting paradox and ambiguity as common rather than as aberrations.

All of us have accumulated considerable knowledge over our lifetimes. Many times this old knowledge helps us deal with new situations. As we face a new challenge, we recall similar situations in our past, and we apply what we have learned to the new situation. Unfortunately, much of the knowledge—skills, attitudes, facts, values, and beliefs—that we have accumulated does not fit the new and novel situations we are now facing. In fact, this old knowledge often *prevents* us from confronting unusual situations in new ways. We attempt to make our old knowledge fit the new situation. Sometimes it does, and we move forward happily. But often our old knowledge does not fit, and we are frustrated and keep trying our old solutions in new situations and consistently see them fail. Here is where the concept of unlearning fits. When learning something new, we must contend with the old knowledge that we already have. We can't merely pull some magical plug and allow the old knowledge to drain away so we can replace it with what is new.

Related to the canoe trip described above, one of the participants was visibly upset that the printed schedule had been changed because of the thunderstorm. He said, "So what if some of us are a little wet and a few tents are ruined? We said we were going to canoe for four days, and we should canoe for that many days. When a plan is made, we should stick to it."

He wrestled with a set of beliefs he had that plans, once carefully thought through and written, should not be modified. His unlearning involved setting aside these beliefs and adjusting plans as circumstances dictated. He had to unlearn the idea that original plans were always better than contingency plans. Several months later he still talked about the canoe trip and the change in plans. He continued to unlearn. Unlearning often takes time.

Unlearning means examining old knowledge in light of present situations and then dealing with both the content and the associated feelings. Unlearning is a transformation process (see Chapter Eleven) in which old knowledge is examined, feelings are dealt with, some old knowledge is brought forward, and some is set aside and replaced.

Without attending to unlearning and the transformation that accompanies it, many people are stuck in their struggles with new situations. Often they aren't aware of why they are having such difficulty adjusting to new situations. For example, supervisors often feel frustrated when persons they are helping don't catch on. It's possible that neither the supervisor (teacher) nor the learner is aware that old knowledge is in the way and that some attention must be paid to unlearning the old before progress can be made with the new.

Individuals learn and unlearn not only for their own benefit but also to change and renew communities and organizations. Peter Senge (1990) makes a strong case for learning organizations, which are, he writes, "organizations where people continually expand their capacity to create the results they truly desire, where new and expansive patterns of thinking are nurtured, where collective aspiration is set free, and where people are continually learning how to learn together" (p. 3).

Beliefs and values are the cornerstone for learning in the emerging age—beliefs and values of teachers, of learners, and of organizations. Identifying beliefs and values, examining them, and dealing with the feelings associated with them is often the key to unlearning. For instance, if we believe that older people cannot learn as effectively as younger people and we have some old research data to support this view, we may have difficulty accepting a situation where older people are viewed as equally competent as younger learners. We may even have new research that refutes the old position. Yet we still hold this belief, perhaps unknowingly, that older people can't learn as well. Here is a case where some unlearning is necessary, and it may well start with updated research information. Such information may not be sufficient, particularly if the person has deeply ingrained beliefs and perhaps some personal experience that reinforces their views.

Other Considerations

Ideas from Eastern and Western thought are commingling and providing us with new ideas about education and leadership. As Fritjof Capra (1991), a physicist, points out, "One of the strongest parallels to Eastern mysticism has been the realization that the constituents of matter and the basic phenomena involving them are all interconnected; that they cannot be understood as isolated entities but only as integral parts of a unified whole." Capra continues, "The universe, in fact, may be interconnected in much subtler ways than one had thought before. The new kind of interconnectedness that has recently emerged not only enforces the similarities between the views of physicists and mystics; it also raises the intriguing possibility of relating subatomic physics to Jungian psychology and, perhaps, even to parapsychology; and it may shed new light on the fundamental role of probability in quantum physics" (p. 309).

Physicists and biologists have moved past ideas of individualism and competition to ideas of community and cooperation, yet many in education cling to individualism and competition as cornerstones for education. Many educators have great difficulty embracing cooperative learning and the possibility that learning means teachers, knowledge, and learners all working together as part of the learning process. New trends in science, Eastern thought, and Western thought stretch us to think of teaching and learning in new and expanded ways that go well beyond what the current more traditional research and scholarship about education suggest. Capra and others who are working at integrating approaches to knowing that many people thought impossible to integrate give us a glimpse into an entirely new perspective on education.

In the emerging age, we wrestle with the apparent paradox of mixing the rational with the nonrational, the scientific with the artistic, the logical with the mystical. We learn from the writings of Western writers, but we also heed writers from other perspectives. For example, Benjamin Hoff (1992) writes that a Taoist might say, "Carefully observe the natural laws in operation in the world around you, and live by them. From following them, you learn the morality of modesty, moderation, compassion, and consideration (not just one society's rules and regulations), the wisdom of seeing things as they are (not merely collecting 'facts' about them), and the happiness of being in harmony with the Way (which has nothing to do with self-righteous 'spiritual' obsessions and fanaticism). And you will live lightly, spontaneously, and effortlessly" (pp. 155–156). This is useful information for teachers, learners, and leaders.

We are in a time when we must view who we are and what we do in a global context. Walter Anderson (1990) says that we are seeing "the birth of a global culture, with a worldview that is truly a *world* view. Globalization provides a new arena (or theater) in which all belief systems look around and become aware of other belief systems, and in which people everywhere struggle in unprecedented ways to find out who and what they are" (p. 6). He also says, "In a global—and globalizing—era, all of the old structures of political reality, all the old ways of saying who we are and what we are for and what we are against, seem to be melting into air" (p. 231).

Thinking globally also means considering teaching and learning in broader, more expansive ways. For instance, being aware of multiple belief systems and the variety of information systems implied by them forces teachers to rethink their views of information and the value of context in teaching and learning.

In an extremely impoverished community in the mountains adjacent to Mexico City, a group of local people operate a community center. The community combines health care functions for all ages, nutrition education for pregnant women, day-care facilities for those employed in Mexico City, and educational programs on child care. A dentist, a medical technician, and a community development worker make up the staff. At various times each of them teaches in one or more of the programs, along with many volunteers from the community who assist. One day they may teach children, another day adults. Much of their teaching is through home visits as they help families cope with inadequate nutrition and bad water.

These community educators have little to work with, yet the results of their efforts are reflected in the stories told by the people who have participated in the programs. The most poignant stories are about people who feel that they now have some control over their lives and their community through the efforts of this modest little community center.

As we move into the emerging age, new thinking begins to surface about what knowledge is and how it is structured, what learning is and how it occurs, who teachers are and what they do, and a host of other considerations. Just as the emerging age leaves behind many assumptions of the industrial era, so will education leave behind many of its outdated assumptions. Newer assumptions are slowly emerging, allowing all of us who work with adult learning organizations to develop newer and more appropriate perspectives, strategies, and solutions for handling the problems and challenges of the present.

In the next chapter we begin discussing approaches that leaders can follow in taking charge of their own leadership development.

Chapter Ten

A Personal Approach to Leadership Development

The approach used throughout this book is to expose you to ideas about leadership and to invite you to grapple with them, argue with them, try them out, rethink them, and give them personal relevance. The basic premise is that you are in charge of your own learning and development. This chapter contains suggestions, exercises, and approaches for doing more with the ideas presented here than merely reading about them.

Principles for Taking Charge of Your Development

A number of principles for taking charge of your own learning and development have proved their worth. Here we discuss a wide selection of them.

- *Becoming a leader is a developmental process.* Even if we pay careful attention to the approaches suggested here, we will not immediately become more highly qualified leaders.

- *Leadership development is an ongoing lifelong process.* None of us will ever achieve our absolute fullest potential. We will continue to learn throughout our lives. We may now hold leadership positions, perhaps highly responsible ones, yet we must continue to learn and develop.

- *We are the most important teacher for developing leadership capacity in ourselves.* We are responsible for our own learning. No one knows what we already know. No one knows better than we do what we ought to learn. Assessment forms provide only a glimpse into what we already know and can do. What our supervisor or some expert believes we ought to learn may or may not truly be what we should learn. Assessment forms, supervisors, and experts have a place in our learning in that often we are unaware of what we ought to learn, and such outside approaches can be of help in gaining this awareness. What is key, though, is that we remain in charge of our learning and not blindly accept everything that an assessment instrument or some other person says.

• *Spending time reviewing the body of research about leaders and leadership provides an insufficient basis for our learning.* Much of the research about leadership involves identifying "successful" leaders in various positions. Researchers ask these leaders to complete various kinds of instruments. The researchers assume that every successful leader must have the skills, knowledge, and attitudes of the leaders in their study. Under rapidly changing conditions, skills and knowledge that work with today's organizations often will not work for tomorrow's. Further, much of this research takes a rather mechanistic approach to leadership, assuming that what is important about leadership can be codified and measured. Many of today's successful leaders argue that what is important is more than a series of measurable skills, a list of traits, and a body of knowledge. These leaders often talk about the artful dimensions of leadership, about values and beliefs, about feelings. The reasons for their success go well beyond the visible and measurable. Someone once said that truth is like a butterfly: one can examine all of its pieces and even construct a replica, but the essence of the butterfly is its life, and that defies measurement or construction. Thus it is with leadership research and leadership assessment instruments. We can learn something about the pieces of leadership, but what is most important defies simple measurement.

Also, to take the butterfly example a step further, we may take a butterfly apart and attempt to reconstruct it—but the situation may require not a butterfly but an antelope. So we lose in both respects. We cannot construct a living butterfly, nor, in many instances, is it a butterfly that we should be attempting to construct.

- *Our personal histories influence greatly what we already know and what we are readily able to learn.* Examining our personal histories can help us immeasurably as we attempt to make sense out of who we are and why we think and act as we do (some approaches for getting in touch with your personal history will be presented shortly).

- *Our beliefs and values are fundamental to our development as leaders.* Identifying what we believe and what we value is basic to our learning. (See Chapters Four and Five for suggestions for identifying personal beliefs and values.)

- *We develop as leaders through a variety of means.* Formal workshops and courses are one way. Our own reading, talking with others, writing about our experiences, and trying out new ideas are at least equally valuable and often more so than what is gained in more formal learning.

- *As leaders for the emerging age, we must put known leadership knowledge and guidelines into perspective.* Skills and knowledge are important and often useful, but a leader's personal philosophy of leadership is far more important and far more applicable when the leader confronts situations for which no known skills and no known checklist apply. We must move beyond merely developing skills and accumulating knowledge. In addition to many other facets, our learning encompasses making meaning from our life histories and our experiences and from the information, insights, and perspectives that we encounter. For many of us, learning involves a transformation as we bring old ideas and long-standing beliefs, information, and attitudes into question, examine them, and then often modify or leave them behind. Unlearning, and the transformation that is involved in doing it, is a profound kind of learning for many of us (see Chapter Eleven).

• *As leaders, we must conceive of learning in at least two ways: (1) learning something and then later applying the learning and (2) learning as we are doing—that is, learning a skill as we practice it.* Many leadership situations require skills that apply only to that one, unique situation. We track the situation constantly and invent appropriate skills as we apply them. More often than not, we may then toss this newly learned skill on the leader skill junk heap because the chances of using it again are slim.

• *We must come to appreciate that we learn both alone and in community with others.* Unfortunately, many of us are neither alone nor in community. (We discuss solitude and community further below.)

• *Not all learning is pleasurable.* As we uncover old memories, question long-held beliefs, challenge perspectives, and recognize that certain skills no longer work, pain and despair result. This discomfort can jar us from old ways of thinking and doing. We replace the pain of the moment with new perspectives, new skills, new truth that results in positive feelings. Unfortunately, some of us allow ourselves to be so engulfed by these negative feelings that we don't learn our way out and instead wallow in despair. As leaders, we must recognize that our lives will include moments of unhappiness but that these moments can be keys to learning and change.

• *All of us have personal demons that we try to avoid.* Demons are things, imagined or real, that cause distress and anxiety and interfere with our becoming what we are capable of becoming. Insecurity and worry are demons; so are fear of failure and its other face, reluctance to take risks. All of us have a head full of demons, and they have likely plagued us for years. Many of our demons are obviously negative: fear, lack of confidence, shyness. But some of our worst demons may be what we consider positive features of our lives. Overconfidence and its close cousin, arrogance, are demons.

Success is a demon. Some of us fear success. We wonder how success will affect us and whether the negative aspects of success may be more powerful than the positive. We have observed what success seems to have done to certain people's lives, and we don't want that to happen to us. Success is also a demon if it prevents us from striking out in new directions.

Tradition is a demon. Depending on others for direction, waiting for someone to act before we do, and blaming others for our failed actions are demons. Our expertness can be a demon, particularly if it closes us to new learning and new experiences. Power is often a demon for leaders.

The so-called fraud syndrome is a demon for many of us, particularly if we have just been appointed to a new leadership position. In the quiet moments following the good news of our appointment and any ensuing celebration, we begin to think about our new position. Questions and doubts pop into our consciousness: Will I be able to do this job? Do I have the necessary qualifications? If the selection committee really knew me, it probably wouldn't have selected me. Am I a fraud for even applying for this position? Will I ever really be worth the salary they plan to pay me? Surely there are people more qualified than I am for this position. It goes on and on. This wave of self-doubt in the face of success may sound silly to someone who has never experienced it, but feeling unworthy is a demon that even many competent people face.

You might want to take time right now to make a list of your demons. Listing them is a good way to began dealing with them. What do we do with demons? Ignore them? That is a common response. Many of us recognize our demons and learn to live with them, realizing that they often cause agony in our lives and sometimes prevent us from doing what we might otherwise do. Occasionally our demons work so subtly that we believe we are performing to our full capacity when we are not. We listened to a demon and quit a task early; we failed to search for the most creative response; we depended on the knowledge we had on hand; we accepted someone else's ideas without question; and so on.

Parker Palmer (1990) writes of an experience he had in the Outward Bound program. He feared most the challenge of roping himself down a 110-foot cliff. The instructions were clear—he should lean back, supported by a rope, and then "walk" down the cliff. The natural inclination was to hug the cliff, not lean away from it. Halfway down the cliff he froze. The instructor waited an eternity, according to Palmer's recollection, before she said anything. Then she yelled up to him, "If you can't get out of it, get into it." And so he got into it and his feet began to move.

Palmer (1990) refers to demons as monsters. He writes, "We must sometimes ride the monsters all the way down. Some monsters simply will not go away. They are too big to walk around, too powerful to overcome, too clever to outsmart. The only way to deal with them is to move toward them, with them, into them, through them" (p. 33).

Confronting demons is a risky proposition. Demons wouldn't be demons if they weren't so powerful, pervasive, and enduring. Not confronting your demons and allowing them to control who you are and what you do is giving them too much power. Take them on. Confront them. Learn to walk on the side of the cliff. Confront your demons by doing the opposite of what common sense may tell you to do. If common sense says hug the wall, try leaning away from it. If fear of failure often prevents you from trying something that you would like to try, try it anyway. Look forward to the failure and be willing to accept it. What often results is no failure at all, and you have moved one step toward slaying a notorious demon.

One easy and often positive way to confront your demons, once you have listed them, is to begin writing about them in your journal. Taking a demon out of your head and putting it on paper can often defang it. (Several ideas for journal writing are suggested later in this chapter.)

Developing a Learning Plan

A learning plan, even though it will change almost from the moment you begin trying to carry it out, is a systematic way to assess where you are and where you want to go in learning about leaders, leadership, and organizations. Learning to develop a learning plan—in other words, learning how to be systematic in planning one's own learning—can help in confronting the emerging age. As we increasingly face stormy-weather leadership situations, we must not only take charge of our learning but effectively plan it.

This is a new idea for many people. Most of us have spent years attending courses, classes, and workshops that have been planned by others. We have not had to map out our own plan. Now the situation is such that we must learn to do this, do it well, and do it often.

Realize, too, as I emphasized earlier, that a learning plan cannot prepare us for all stormy-weather leadership requirements. A learning plan can help build the capacity each leader needs to face an unknown future where many of today's leadership skills are irrelevant. Much of a leader's learning occurs on the job, while facing problems and challenges that develop each day.

A Personal Learning Plan

Here I present the components for developing a personal learning plan. You may want to add features to the plan, and some items listed here may not fit who you are and how you want to plan your learning. If so, modify the suggested plan to fit your own personal situation.

1. *Describe the context in which you work as a leader.* Describe, briefly, the main elements of the organization in which you work. What is its primary mission? Where do you fit in the organization?

What are you expected to do? Are there particular characteristics of the organization that require you to act in unique ways—expected communication patterns, for example? (See Chapter Four for an in-depth discussion of context and how to appraise it.)

2. *Describe who you are as a leader.* Write about the things you do well as a leader and feel positive about, as well as the things you do less well and want to improve on. Your statement should cover skills and knowledge but should also encompass something about your attitudes and feelings concerning leading and being a leader. You may want to do a systematic assessment of your leadership qualities, skills, and knowledge in this section. Most of us know more about leadership than we think we know. Doing an assessment is one way to uncover some of this buried knowledge. (Some ideas for an informal but effective personal leadership assessment are presented later.)

3. *Indicate your long-range goals for yourself as a leader.* You may want to include appropriate personal credo statements as a part of your long-range goals (three to five years hence). (See Chapter Four for a discussion of personal credos and how to write them.)

4. *Indicate a topic you want to learn more about.* It could be a very specific topic such as becoming acquainted with recent research on how organizations are becoming smaller. Or it could be a broader and longer-range topic such as learning more about the role of spirituality in leadership. Your choice of topics may relate to points 1, 2, and 3. Or you may want to reach out beyond your present context and explore broader ideas about leadership. For instance, you may choose as a topic "approaches to sharing power in an organization." Your topic could be an area in which you believe you fall short and want to improve, or it could be an area in which you are already strong but want to become stronger.

5. *Write one or more learning objectives or learning themes for each topic.* For the more specific topics, your objectives or themes can

be more specific (exactly what you want to learn or to be able to do). For the more general and farther-reaching topics, your objectives or themes can be less specific. In some cases, when you want to learn more about a big topic on which you now know little, you may indicate a direction for your learning and not worry about making it sound like a learning objective.

Learning objectives or themes related to the topic "approaches to sharing power in an organization" might include these:

To update myself on new research and scholarship about power in modern organizations

To discover examples in organizations where attempts have been made to share power

To develop specific strategies for sharing power

Seldom is it possible to plan thoroughly what to learn before the learning begins. Hence, firm, predetermined learning objectives can be millstones as well as road markers; it depends on how they are used. It is like traveling on a road enshrouded in fog. You think you're on the right road, but when the fog clears, you know the road is not right and you search for another, or you leave the well-traveled paths entirely, searching for your own trail. Learning objectives and themes are a way to begin taking charge of your learning. But they are best used as temporary guides rather than as permanent markers.

Also, don't overlook the learning that occurs that you didn't plan for. Sometimes the unplanned learning becomes the most important lesson, if you are open to it. You may have a hunch about something you want to learn but can't put it into words. Don't worry about the words—what you are learning is far more important than carefully crafted learning objectives.

6. *List the approaches and resources that will help you attain your learning objectives or themes.* Examples of resources are books,

books, credit courses, noncredit courses, workshops, conferences, colleagues in your organization, persons outside your organization, videotapes, audiotapes, computer programs, journal and magazine articles, on-line computer databases, and visits to other organizations.

For example, to meet the first objective in our example, you might discover a workshop on sharing power at a nearby college or university and sign up for it. You could do a computer data search that might lead you to several new books on sharing power.

It is also useful to indicate the dates when you plan to complete work on each learning objective or theme. We all know that none of us will ever completely meet a learning objective, but setting a date provides a sense of urgency and adds a little discipline to our efforts.

For some topics, you may not know what you do not know and consequently have difficulty defining what resources can assist you. To solve this dilemma, a good place to start your learning is with someone who knows something about the topic and can direct you to the appropriate resources. Thus you may complete your learning plan in stages. You might do a preliminary plan in which you indicate the topics you want to learn and the general objectives you want to attain or the direction you want to take. As you become better acquainted with the topic by talking with others, attending workshops, and so on, you may learn about additional resources. You may also discover that your learning objectives were the wrong ones and write a new set. Thus, developing a learning plan is a dynamic rather than a fixed, linear process.

7. *Include progress indicators*. What indicators will let you know what you are accomplishing and what remains to be accomplished? For example, at one level you could say that you plan to keep a list of all books read, all videotapes viewed, and all workshops attended, and to write a brief statement in your journal about what

you learned and how you reacted to the ideas, approaches, and suggestions. Depending on what you are learning, you could also mention indicators related to how you plan to try what you are learning in your work.

Keeping a Journal

Recently, I led a weeklong national workshop for extension deans and directors. I asked them to keep a journal during the workshop. After I had talked about what was involved and passed out blank journal books, I asked for response.

One fairly open fellow from North Dakota said, "I grew up thinking that keeping a diary was kind of a sissy thing that teenage girls did."

His reaction is a common one. However, journaling is not keeping a diary, particularly in the way that some of us remember writing in a diary when we were ten years old. Most diaries of our youth were calendar books with a few blank lines for each date. That was it. Unfortunately, many people continue to think of journals as childhood diaries.

In almost every workshop I teach, I discover several people who are longtime journal writers. They are quick to share the benefits they have gotten from regular writing.

I have kept a journal for more than twenty-five years, one in which I write nearly every day. Journaling has helped me in several ways:

• *To discover what I know that I am not aware of knowing.* I am not always aware of what I know about how I lead and how I teach. By writing regularly in my journal, I've found that I can often uncover some of this hidden knowledge. Sometimes the uncovering of hidden knowledge, even though I might never use it, is itself a satisfying and confidence-building activity.

- *To clarify a problem or a situation I am facing.* During the years I worked as an administrator, seldom a day went by in which I didn't encounter a problem that at first appeared impossible to resolve. (Sometimes the many dimensions of a problem were almost incomprehensible, particularly when first introduced.) When I faced these puzzlelike problems, I usually took time to write about them in my journal. Almost always, as I began writing about the problem, its essence became clearer to me, and alternative solutions began popping into my head.

- *To confront my personal demons.*

- *To create new ideas.* Sometimes, when I am writing in my journal, a new idea will pop into my head. For me, as for many people, the process of writing is an idea stimulator. I come to my journal not quite sure what I'm going to write about, and as I begin writing, ideas began flowing, one building on another. I have been surprised at the words appearing on the page. Sometimes they seem to appear almost mysteriously.

In another workshop where participants were journaling, one woman seemed reluctant and more than a little skeptical about journal writing. She confessed that she hadn't written in a "diary" since she was thirteen years old.

At breakfast on the second day, I asked her how it was going. With a sparkle in her eye, she replied, "Much better than I ever expected. In fact, I couldn't sleep this morning, so I got up early and began writing in my journal, just to see what might happen."

"What happened?" I inquired.

"I don't really know," she said, smiling. "The pen was moving so fast, I've got to go back to my room to see what it said."

She had experienced what many journal writers experience once they begin writing: they are surprised at what flows from their pens.

- *To tie action to reflection.* Most administrative leaders, myself included, are long on action and short on reflection. We know how to do things, and we pride ourselves on the results of our efforts. Yet often our actions would be improved if we took more time to reflect—to consider what happened when we acted, why we believe it happened, and what we believe we would do differently another time, or even more radical, to consider that certain actions shouldn't have been done at all, even if they appeared to work well. As leaders, we must continually reflect on what we are doing and even ask if we should continue doing certain things. (We will return to this topic shortly.)

- *To sort out what is important.* Journal writing is a valuing process. What you choose to write about is what you, at least at that moment, believe has highest value. People who have kept journals for several years find it interesting to go back and review what they wrote. For instance, in my own journal writing, I start each entry with a brief mention of the weather. This traces back to my days growing up on a farm where everything we did was closely tied to the weather. I also grew up during the Great Depression, so I have always been concerned about family finances, much to the exasperation and frustration of my children. My journals record what we paid for automobiles, what the children's college tuition cost, and so on. The problems from work I chose to write about said something about the problems that were most important to me, even though I'm sure that at the time I saw many of them as thorns that I wished would disappear.

After writing in a journal for a few months, it is interesting to go back and read what you chose to write about. Your choices, no matter what you wrote, say much about what you value.

- *To create a permanent record.* When you write in your journal, you are writing history. You can return to it again and again and see what you thought, what you did, and how you did it (depending, of course, on what your journals contain). I include a lot of what I would consider historical material in my journals. For example, I note down the books I read each year, including the publication details and a short book review.

I record all my trips—where I went, when, and for what purpose. I record family happenings—my daughter's wedding, job changes—both happy events and disasters that befall us. I include the joyful and the sad, the disappointments and the successes—as I define them.

• *To make meaning.* For many journal keepers, myself included, journal writing helps make meaning of life. As we write about what we do, think, and feel and our reactions to these things, we are making meaning. As we wend our way through the transformation process (see Chapter Eleven), journaling will help us discover meaning in the course of our life changes.

• *To touch our spiritual being.* As we make meaning, we begin to touch the spiritual side of our lives, the deeper, more profound dimensions of our beings. As discussed in Chapter Four, deep within each of us is a spiritual self that gives direction and foundation to our lives. Journal writing is one way to get in touch with our spiritual self and to nourish it.

Tips for Journaling

Here are a few tips for beginning your journal writing endeavor.

Technical Matters

Select a notebook—a blank hardcover book, a loose-leaf notebook to which you can easily add pages, or a student's notebook. What you write in is a personal choice and doesn't matter. For many years

I have used hardcover books as journals; earlier, I used loose-leaf notebooks.

I write in longhand in my journal, with either a fountain pen or a felt-tipped pen. For many people, writing in their journal becomes a special, almost sacred activity. They believe that writing in longhand is the only authentic way to record one's thoughts, ideas, and feelings. Others use a word processor to produce neatly printed material, or simply leave the material on a disk. The form really doesn't matter; it's a personal decision.

When should you write? Like so many other things in life, if you plan a regular time for journal writing into your busy schedule, it will happen. If you wait for the "right time," it won't. Some people write for half an hour in the early morning, one of their first activities of the day. Others write at day's end, just before retiring. Again, it doesn't matter when you write. My experience in working with many journal writers is that establishing a regular time is all that matters.

Getting Started

How should you get started? Write the date and the time for each entry. Then if you're stuck and don't know what to write or you are concerned that it won't sound profound enough—these are writers' demons—try one (or all) of the following:

• *Do some "timed writing."* Set a timer for five minutes and began writing. Write whatever comes into your mind, and keep writing until the buzzer rings. You will probably be surprised at what you have said.

• *Try "freewriting."* Freewriting is something like priming a pump. You write, and as you write you think of what to write (to this extent freewriting is similar to timed writing). Freewriting does more than merely help us think of things to write about. Most of us have been taught to plan what we are going to write, to think it through carefully before setting pen to paper or fingers to keyboard. Many of us have been taught to outline what we're going to say, particularly if what we plan to write will run to more than a page or so.

Freewriting allows for a different kind of expression than writing that is carefully planned. William Zinsser (1988), a noted writer and writing teacher, says that freewriting "is a voyage of discovery into the self. Only by going into uncharted territory . . . can a writer find his [or her] potential and . . . voice and . . . meaning. Meaning, in fact, doesn't exist until a writer goes looking for it" (p. 56).

A more focused approach to freewriting is to take a topic—a leadership problem, a person, a demon, a happening—and just write about it, putting down whatever comes into your mind.

• *Write letters.* Assume that you are writing to someone when you write in your journal. This often helps the process considerably, for most of us are somewhat accustomed to writing letters. John Steinbeck, the famed novelist, was a regular journal writer. In the journal he kept while writing the novel *East of Eden*, Steinbeck wrote a daily letter to his literary agent—except he never mailed the letters.

• *Write dialogue.* Dialogue involves more than one voice, of course. One way is to write a letter to someone and then write a response, as if the other person were actually answering the letter.

Another way is to write as if you were holding a conversation with someone. You say something, the person responds to you (of course, you are writing what you expect the person would say), you speak again, you get a response, and so on.

Yet another approach is to establish mythical characters that represent different parts of yourself. For example, we each have a creative self and a judging self. We might write a conversation between the creator and the judge that would go something like this:

> *Creator:* I've just thought of a new way to reorganize our unit so that more people can have responsibility for their own decision making. I've got to try out the idea on a few people, particularly some of those who will be directly affected.
>
> *Judge:* Why don't you just leave well enough alone? You're always coming up with new ideas—look what happened to the last restructuring idea you had! Nobody would go along with it. And besides, what makes you think those people you supervise want any more responsibility for what they do? They seem happy just the way they are.

The conversation would continue, back and forth.

Writing dialogue not only allows you to put your thoughts and feelings on paper; it also encourages you to take another person's perspective. By doing so, you often learn things about yourself that you didn't know before.

A Window on Your Personal History

Where you were born, who your parents were, where you went to school, your home neighborhood, and who your friends were have had and continue to influence what you know, how you learn, and nearly all other aspects of your life. Reflecting on your life stories and your history is a starting point for understanding who you are.

No matter how much some of us would like to ignore or change portions of our personal histories, they define who we are. This does not mean that we must accept how we relate to our histories. After we have identified elements of our personal histories, we can choose how we wish to relate to them. As Richard Bach (1977) observed, "You're always free to change your mind and choose a different future, or a different past" (p. 51). One way to open a window on our personal histories is to construct a road map of our lives lived so far.

- Turn a piece of paper horizontal, and in the left bottom corner write your date of birth. Start drawing a line, upward and toward the right. Try to recall crossroads in your life, and mark them on your map. For instance, entering first grade may have been a crossroad; indicate it. Your first love may have been a crossroad, your first job for pay, the first time you got an F, and so on.

- Identify one person in your life that you believe made a great difference. Describe this person in your journal, recalling as much detail as you can. Also write about the major contributions that you believe this person made to your life.

- Make a list of firsts—the first thing you remember, your first day of school, your first friend, your first major illness, your first job, and so on.

- On a large piece of paper, using a felt-tipped pen, draw the events, people, and places that made the most difference in your life. Then, in your journal, write about the images you drew.

- Draw the floor plan for the house or apartment in which you grew up. If you grew up in several, select one that had the most meaning for you. Draw in the furniture, show the pictures on the walls and the clocks, books, and other items in their appropriate places. Put people in the rooms. Jot down the smells and sounds associated with each room. Indicate the feelings that you recall as you move from room to room.

Having done these various exercises, several of which are designed to tap your unconscious, reflect on what you have done. Do threads of information emerge from the various exercises? Are you able to detect themes of feelings, beliefs, and values in what you are remembering?

This preliminary personal history work can provide you with the beginnings of perspectives that you will find especially valuable as you attempt to learn more about yourself as a person and work toward development as a leader.

Solitude and Community

We learn by ourselves, and we learn when we are with others. Some of us prefer one approach over the other. Nevertheless, each approach has an important contribution to make to our learning and development as leaders.

Many of us, it seems, experience neither solitude nor community. We hover somewhere in between. Many of us are around people all the time. Our lives are filled with people. But community means more than having a people-filled life. Some of us, in the quiet of evening, are alone. But solitude is more than being alone, just as community is more than being with other people.

Solitude is a settling time, a time for us to confront ourselves, to listen for the whispers in our lives that are masked by the shouts of others and our own loud voices. In solitude we confront the emptiness of silence as we listen for the whispers and hear nothing because our inner voices have been muffled by the deafening roar of our often frantic everyday lives.

Solitude is a way for us to get in touch with our spiritual selves, to touch our souls. In solitude we discover our personal truths, more profound than all the great truths of the experts.

In solitude we get in touch with ourselves, who we are, what we believe, and what we value. Palmer (1983) says, "If knowledge allows us to receive the world as it is, solitude allows us to receive ourselves as we are" (p. 121).

Experiencing solitude can be frightening, especially for people who seldom do. Sometimes, in the depths of solitude, we are bored and we wish that someone, anyone, would talk to us. At other times we are profoundly afraid and disappointed because we do not like the self we find.

I have a cabin in a sparsely settled region in central Wisconsin some thirty-five miles from any city. Several times each year I go alone to my cabin, for two to five days at a time. The cabin is located on a hundred acres of rolling land, some of it former farmland but much of it now forested. A small, isolated pond huddles on one side of the property where ducks nest, beavers work, and sandhill cranes trumpet their ancient calls.

It is here that I find solitude. It is here that I confront where I have been, where I am, and where I think I'm headed. It is here that I once more introduce myself to me and become reacquainted. It is here that I revisit my personal truths, sometimes discovering new ones, sometimes struggling to rid myself of old ones. It is here where I often do nothing but sit on a hillside in spring, in the midst of acres of orange hawkweed, and allow my mind to go blank. It is here, in the fall, where I sit on the south slope of a hillside, allowing the sun to warm me and the smells of autumn to engulf me. Doing nothing, I am doing much. While I rest, I work, for deep within me a great struggle goes on as feelings, ideas, impressions, and experiences collide.

In solitude my most profound ideas are born and my worst fears are uncovered. In solitude I find great joy and deep sorrow. And I learn.

But solitude is not enough. We also need community, the presence of others to learn. The offhand comment, the wordless expression, and the quick rebuttal give feedback on our ideas. Even if our immediate reaction is defensive and our feelings are negative, we can learn. Other people provide mirrors for us. In these mirrors we see ourselves. It is easy to dismiss our mirrors, particularly those that reflect what we perceive as negatives. We must learn to accept the reflection and try to see and hear, even if our immediate impulse is to reject the image.

Community also means having a few close friends or associates with whom we can share our innermost thoughts and get a reaction that is not judgmental, and to whom we are willing to listen and do the same thing. Community allows us to move deeper into ourselves, even if all we do is describe a leadership situation and know that someone else will hear. In the act of describing, in the presence of at least one other person, a deeper realization of meaning begins to emerge.

Community does not require dozens of people. Community may consist of one other person or perhaps a half dozen others. For the kind of learning I am talking about, smaller groups provide more opportunity than larger groups because there is time for all parties to be heard. There are also time and opportunity for deeper knowing of people.

Sometimes we refer to the one other person with whom we share ideas as a mentor. This is a particular kind of community wherein the inexperienced person works with the more experienced. Much can be learned by both parties in mentor situations.

Community can be effective with peers, too, as long as those involved are willing to listen, perhaps raising questions for understanding but avoiding making judgments or offering suggestions.

Learning of the kind I am suggesting, whereby we explore deeper ideas in the context of ourselves, requires a mix of solitude and community. Both contribute to learning. Although the two approaches may sound contradictory, in reality they are cumulative.

Approaches to Reflection

We can learn much through reflection, purposefully attending to and processing what we are experiencing. Several approaches can help us reflect. As people with whom we work react to what we do and how we do it, we often are pushed into reflecting, perhaps when we had not intended to do so. Other people provide mirrors for us, allowing us to see what we do from another perspective. These mirrors can be valuable triggers for reflection. For example, if people tell us that they wouldn't have made the decision we did and give us several reasons why, we have food for reflection. Another mirror for our thinking and acting is reading material that offers a variety of perspectives on leading and leadership, particularly material that tends to differ with the approaches that we use.

Our own stories are excellent material for reflection and can provide in-depth information about how we lead, what works and doesn't work, and who we are and what we believe and value.

Reflecting on Our Stories

Start by writing three leadership stories. Think back over the last six months, and recall three kinds of leadership situations:

1. What situation or incident in your role as an administrative leader caused you the greatest happiness, pleasure, or satisfaction?
2. What situation or incident caused you the most strife, anxiety, or pain?
3. What situation was totally unplanned and may have caught you completely off guard, yet you were required to exercise leadership immediately, without any preparation time?

In no more than a page or two, write a description of what happened in each of these situations. Be sure to give details:

- When and where did the event occur?
- What was the context for the event? Had something occurred that led up to this event? What was it? Was the event a surprise to you, or had you seen it coming?

- Who were the people involved (not names but roles or positions)? What did each of them do?
- What key dimensions of the event made it particularly pleasurable or particularly troublesome for you? Why?
- Exactly how did you respond to the event? What did you do immediately? What did you do later?
- What feelings did you have during and after the event? Be as specific as you can in recounting them.

To reflect as honestly as you can about each of these situations, you may want to set aside your feelings for the moment and not allow them to influence your recollection of what happened. Sometimes particularly strong feelings, especially negative ones, prevent us from reconstructing a situation accurately. One way of setting aside feelings is to confront them openly by listing them.

Once you have written the stories, set them all aside for a day or two, and then read each of them carefully. Ask yourself several questions—and write down the answers. No situation is ever a total success or a total failure, so the same questions are relevant to each situation. If you are comfortable doing so, you might share your written stories with a friend, mentor, colleague, or someone else with whom you are comfortable. Likewise, if colleagues with whom you are comfortable were participants in the same situation, you might ask them to respond to these questions without reading your stories. By involving other people, you are able to gain a perspective that is beyond your own.

For your own analysis of each story, write answers to the following questions:

1. In each situation, what went well? Why do you think it went well? What did you do to contribute to the situation's success? Be as specific as you can. Was it something that you

knew, some skill that you had, or some perspective that you had gained that you believe made the difference? What exactly?

2. What resulted from this situation? Was something accomplished? What? Why was it accomplished? Was it an accident? Something you or someone else did? Something else? In each situation, do you believe that something different might have happened if you had done something differently? What?

3. In each situation, what didn't go well? Why do you think it didn't go well? What do you think you did or didn't do that caused it to go poorly? Be as specific as you can.

4. List the skills, knowledge, perspectives, and attitudes that you possess that you believe were important in each situation.

5. In similar fashion, list areas where you believe you can improve.

6. What feelings do you now have about each of these situations? Have there been any changes from your earlier feelings?

Outside Interests

A few years ago I invited a resource person to explain to a group how he found time to do everything that he did in his busy life. This man was a well-known leader in his field, and everyone in the group had read at least one of his books. I imagine people expected him to talk about how he organized his life, how he managed his time, and how he set priorities in his work. He didn't talk about any of these things.

"What all of us need," he said, "is to take time to cultivate interests outside of our work."

The group stared at him, I suspect not clearly understanding what he was saying. He went on to explain how important it was, in his opinion, to lead a balanced life, to work hard at what one does but also to leave work regularly to do other things.

Many leaders I know fail in this regard. They have become so engulfed in their work that they have lost touch with their outside interests, if they had any. They become single-track people.

I once did a study on outstanding leaders in adult education. After a selection process that identified these persons, I interviewed each of them in their home cities. Each and every one of them had engaging outside interests. One woman I talked with owned her own airplane and flew regularly; one man was a concert pianist (proficient enough to have performed professionally); another man was an avid trout fisherman; another was a candy maker. Some had multiple interests—for example, the candy maker was also into canoeing, hiking, and gardening.

Each of these people spoke highly of the need to leave one's work from time to time and become immersed in something else. Every one of these people said that time away from work enhanced their work, in addition to making them feel more whole as a person.

Taking charge of your own development is key to becoming a leader for the emerging age. As you become involved in various leadership development activities, you will discover something that you probably learned long ago: personal change can be both joyful and sad. In the next chapter, I will examine the transformation process.

Chapter Eleven

The Transformation
Process

As leaders attempt to adjust their leadership approaches to the requirements of the emerging age, most will experience transformation. Transformation is much more than change. It is an enhancement of personal reality, as well as a conversion of reality. It is a psychological process, an emotional experience, and an encounter that touches the soul. It is a venture that leaves behind old ideas, perspectives, attitudes, beliefs, and approaches, and mourns their loss. It is a process that celebrates endings and anticipates beginnings. Within the process are elements of great joy and celebration and dimensions of great sadness and despair.

The transformation process that I describe here involves a rational, analytic side, particularly in the early stages. At the same time, the process involves an emotional side that is nonrational and nonanalytic. The emotional side is expressed in feelings rather than in facts, in passion rather than in deliberation. This emotional dimension of transformation comes from the heart rather than from the mind, from the soul rather than from the intellect.

Transformation begins for many of us with a situation that we examine and analyze. But once we are into the process, it quickly moves into deeper dimensions. For example, in developing a personal philosophy of leadership (described in Chapters Four and Five), I ask people to look into their personal histories. In examining my own personal history, the following facts I recorded include the following:

Born during the Great Depression of the 1930s

Raised on a sandy farm in north-central Wisconsin without electricity, indoor plumbing, or central heat

Attended a one-room country school where I was the only student in my class (no electricity until I was in the sixth grade)

Contracted polio in the eighth grade, which resulted in paralysis of a leg for more than a year

As I record the facts of my childhood, the feelings well up. Growing up without electricity had a profound influence on who I am today. My town friends who attended high school with me never knew what it was like to read by a dim kerosene lamp. They never knew the deep darkness that enveloped the countryside on a moonless night. They seldom, if ever, experienced the joy of horizon-to-horizon stars that punched mysterious holes in the darkness of the night. Alternately, I felt superior and inferior to my friends who lived in town.

During the years of recovery from polio, I felt great loneliness and profound feelings of self-pity when my friends were participating in sports and I was on the sidelines—despite my relatives' reassurances that I was "fortunate to be alive." The facts of our lives are descriptions, information for the record. The feelings of our lives are windows into the depth of our being, into the soul, into who we are.

When we do a rational analysis—and it is appropriate that we do so in the transformation process—we describe the facts and present information about a situation. Such facts usually lend themselves to listing, with appropriate descriptive and supporting information.

When we incorporate the feeling dimension into our inquiry, we are challenged to use a different form of communication. Listing feelings and emotions can be a beginning, but generally it falls far short of communicating the depth of what we feel. Writing journal entries that probe the many dimensions of our feelings can be a powerful technique. A story or an in-depth description of a critical incident can also be a useful premise for communicating feelings. Such a story should include descriptions of (1) the setting—where the event occurred, what the surroundings were like; (2) the people involved—who they were, what they said, their manner of speaking, and how were they dressed; (3) the context— staff meeting, chance encounter in the hall, session in your office with an unhappy staff person; and (4) what happened—who did what and what resulted.

The emotional side of transformation, in addition to requiring a different form of communication, also proceeds quite differently from rational inquiry. Rational inquiry is linear; one starts at the beginning and proceeds from here to there. The emotional side of transformation may start anywhere and move anywhere or not at all. Often the emotional part of transformation comes when we least expect it. We don't always deliberately say, "Now I must consider the emotional side of what I am doing." But sometimes we do take time to remind ourselves of our feelings and our need to take time to express them.

At times our feelings are not clear. Something nags at us, but we can't put our finger on what it is. During these times, journal writing can help us discover the source of our anguish.

The Transformation Process

Most leaders experience transformation as they attempt to adjust to the requirements of the emerging age. If you are a leader who has become comfortable with more traditional ways of leading— relying on personal power, making top-down decisions, attempting to control the people you supervise, depending on the scientific method for leading, believing that trends and data provide all that is needed for decision making, and subscribing to a host of other beliefs typical of the traditional approach to leadership—you will likely experience a transformation when you begin shifting to leadership approaches for the emerging age.

Becoming a leader for the emerging age involves more than developing a new set of skills and attempting to apply them. Leadership for the emerging age requires, for many leaders, a fundamental shift in beliefs and values about leaders, approaches for leading, people, outcomes for leadership, and the nature of education.

The transformation process (see Figure 11.1) moves through the following phases:

Awareness–analysis

Alternatives

Decision–transition

Action

Although these phases appear linear and straightforward, usually they are not. But awareness is generally the starting point. Some people, when they become aware of a problem, immediately come up with a solution and try it out without spending any time in the other phases. When they do this, they are usually tossed back to the awareness phase, but with either a newer, deeper understanding of it or even greater frustration. Other people move from alternatives to action, trying to avoid the transition phase. However, the transition phase is the core of the process, for that is where the fundamental shifts and changes are made. It is in transition that fundamental transformation occurs.

Also, even though the process phases appear discrete, the whole of the process is represented in each part. For example, the awareness–analysis phase contains elements of the alternative phases, the decision–transition phase, and the action phase. So a

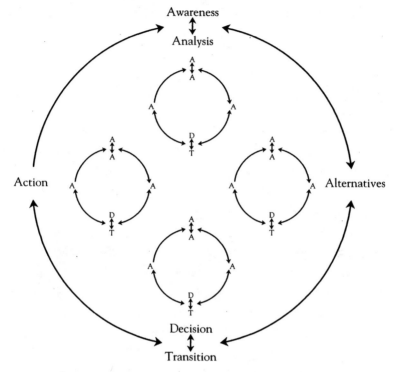

Figure 11.1. The Transformation Process.

transformation occurs within each phase, in addition to an over-riding transformation that encompasses all the phases.

Awareness–Analysis

Let's say you have been an administrative leader for several years. Recently you have become aware that something is wrong. You haven't been able to put your finger on it, but it is a feeling you have. You don't believe you are acting any differently now than you ever did. But a couple of years ago, your unit was humming like a well-oiled machine, whereas today, more often than not it is mis-firing. Complaints are piling up on your desk, from both the people you are supposed to lead and the people who participate in your unit's educational programs.

They say that your unit responds too slowly and that your planning approach is archaic and time-consuming. Your staff complains that you don't give them enough responsibility or sufficient opportunity to do what they are capable of doing. These are the makings of awareness. Transformation can't occur unless you are aware that something needs changing. Until the transformation process begins, you may react to the complaints in a variety of ways: blaming someone or something—another administrator, the lack of budget, the economy, the political party in power. Or you may dismiss the complaints as ill-informed and work hard to satisfy each complaint without examining root causes. Along the way you become angry. How could these people, most of whom you hired, raise these questions with you? And what about the participants in your programs—why are they turning against you? You have difficulty containing your anger at this stage. Still later you attempt to bargain with people who have criticized you and your programs. You ask them, "What can I do to make things better?" And later still you begin feeling that everything is wrong and nothing works anymore. Finally, you accept that something has to change—you, for a start. You will have gone through the same sequence of stages as in grieving, described by Elisabeth Kübler-Ross (1969): denial, anger, bargaining, depression, and acceptance.

The first phase in dealing with a problem, a change, or a situation is to accept the reality of it. Until you reach that point, not much else can happen. A transformation often occurs during the awareness phase. And unless the awareness is accepted and authentic, the remainder of the process will be perfunctory, unimportant, perhaps even detrimental to the situation.

The analysis part of awareness consists of carefully analyzing your situation and the context in which you operate. Examine the complaints you've received. Are there themes? Interview staff members for additional information. Then ask yourself some fundamental questions: What are my assumptions about leaders and leadership? What am I trying to accomplish with my leadership approach? What do I assume about people?

Such an analysis process can be superficial and ultimately not very useful. Or you can open yourself up and allow an internal examination of your fundamental beliefs and values. Such a review is often emotional and heart-wrenching. Unless the analysis moves beyond cold facts into the emotional and feeling stage, it does not provide a sound foundation for transformation. Analysis can and often does lead to considerable unease and pain as you uncover who you are as a leader.

As you become aware of what you value and believe, of how you lead, and of how others view your leadership approach, you may become angry, deny the accuracy of what you are finding out, or become depressed. These emotions are common in the transition phase of transformation.

What you are trying to do in the awareness phase is to get a fix on your own reality. Peter Senge (1990) writes, "An accurate, insightful view of current reality is as important as a clear vision" (p. 155). As you try to become aware, you may also need to examine the forces that prevent you from seeing the truth of your reality. Your personal history, out of which your beliefs and values emerge, influences not only the way in which you see your reality but also which reality becomes a part of your consciousness. Your personal history may block you from becoming aware of what is going on around you, often things that are obvious to others but not to you.

Two strategies can help you become more aware of your reality and help broaden and deepen it. One is to draw a picture of a leadership situation in which you have recently played a part. It could be a meeting with your staff, an encounter with an advisory committee, or a one-to-one meeting with an unhappy part-time instructor. Use stick figures to represent people if that is more comfortable for you. Sketch in as much detail as you can remember.

Once you have drawn the picture, step back and examine it. Do you pick up any clues about your leadership approach from the picture? What about the positions of the people, how they hold their hands, and what they are doing? Do you notice anything from the context of the situation that you drew? Based on these observations, what are your beliefs about people, leaders, and the process of leadership? What values emerge as being most important to you? Do your beliefs and values conflict with what is expected in this leadership situation? Do you need to consider changing any of your beliefs? Which ones? Why? Other questions will likely emerge as you perform this reflective analysis.

Often a picture will reveal nuances of who you are as a leader that may not be evident when you use words to describe what you do. Look for the subtleties in the picture. Consider what you left out of your drawing as well as what you put in. What you left out may provide a powerful clue to who you are as a leader.

A second strategy involves writing. Select another leadership situation, or use the same one for which you drew the picture. This time you will write the "script" of the encounter. Divide the paper into thirds by drawing two lines vertically down the page. Write your conversation in the left column. Write the conversation of all other persons in the right column. As you write your remarks and "hear" the responses, jot your thoughts and feelings in the center column. Try to remember the conversation as accurately as possible, and be honest about the thoughts and feelings you experienced. You'll be surprised at how well you'll be able to do this. Most people find that the details of the event soon come flooding back. When you have completed the exercise, reflect on it by asking the same questions you asked when examining your picture.

Your awareness–analysis work may reveal ambiguity: the situation may still not appear as clear and straightforward as you might like. Leadership situations are often ambiguous and uncertain. As M. Scott Peck (1987) writes, "Those who seek certainty, or who claim certainty in their knowledge, cannot tolerate ambiguity. The word 'ambiguous' means 'uncertain' or 'doubtful,' or capable of being understood in more than one way" (p. 220).

We may view awareness as evolutionary or revolutionary. Our example of things not going well in an organization over time represents evolutionary awareness. Revolutionary awareness comes when we are denied tenure or our adult education department is eliminated or our budget is cut by 20 percent. Revolutionary awareness hits us with little or no warning and hurls us into transformation whether we want it or not. Most of us have experienced both kinds of awareness. It does not matter how we become aware; what matters is that we allow the transformation process to help us work through the ramifications of our awareness.

Alternatives

Once you are aware that something is wrong, that you can't shift blame for it, that a quick fix won't correct it, and that it won't go away if you ignore it, you are ready to move to the alternatives phase of the process.

During this phase you will likely read widely. You may talk with colleagues who seem to be successfully working through the thickets of change and to have developed leadership approaches that work well. As you read and talk and as you reflect on the various leadership alternatives presented, you may find yourself back at the awareness–analysis phase of the process. Using the readings and discussions as mirrors, you begin developing yet another awareness of who you are as a leader and as a person.

One important outcome of the alternatives phase of transformation is finding a variety of approaches to leading. Also in the alternatives phase, at another level, you will discover a variety of beliefs about what it means to lead and what it means to be a leader. You will want to try some of these approaches and avoid others. Some of what you discover will reveal positions similar to those you now hold, but many will likely be considerably different.

Decision–Transition

During this phase of transformation, you begin making decisions about how you want to change. Upon examining your beliefs and values and comparing them with those in the alternatives you have examined, you face decisions. Which of your examined beliefs and values are appropriate for your leadership context, and which are not? What new beliefs do you want to consider that may be more consistent with your leadership context?

For example, you may have believed that unless information and knowledge are scientifically derived, they are not worthy of much consideration. Now you've affirmed that many leaders use an assortment of information and knowledge: scientific research, intuitive ideas, instinct, knowledge gained from experience, and so on. You face modifying your beliefs about information and knowledge.

As you examine your beliefs about people, you may discover that you have considerable faith in people and what they are able to do if given an opportunity. As you make these decisions, some of them obvious, others more subtle, you begin experiencing transition. Transition is the heart of the transformation process. You celebrate the beliefs, values, and ideas that continue to fit your emerging approach to leadership. At the same time, you mourn the loss of old ideas, beliefs, and values that you are leaving behind. The grieving process is very real; losing long-held beliefs and values is very much like losing a loved one.

As William Bridges (1991) points out, "Once you understand that transition begins with letting go of something, you have taken the first step in the task of transition management. The second step is understanding what comes after the letting go: the neutral zone. This is the no-man's land between the old reality and the new. It's the limbo between the old sense of identity and the new. It is a time when the old way is gone and the new doesn't feel comfortable yet" (p. 5).

The neutral zone is a puzzle for most people, particularly for those who are action oriented. These people tend to force their way through the neutral zone, as if logic, study, and hard work will make all the difference. But as Bridges (1991) points out, "This isn't a trip from one side of the street to the other. It is a journey from one identity to the other, and that takes time" (p. 37).

Transition requires time for contemplation. Peck (1987) says, "True contemplation . . . requires meditation. It requires that we stop thinking before we are truly able to think with any original-ity" (p. 211). Contemplation includes emptying the mind or, as Peck says, making room for the "other." This "other" may include "a tale from a strange culture, the different, the unexpected, the new, the better, . . . the other person" (p. 212). Many of us have difficulty "hearing" the "other" because of who we are and where we have been. To quote Peck again, "Unless we empty ourselves of . . . preconceived cultural or intellectual images and expecta-tions, we not only cannot understand the 'other,' we cannot even listen" (p. 214).

Contemplation also includes reflection—on our own experi-ences, on alternatives and possibilities, on what Peck (1987) calls "the unexpected experiences that occur in life and in our relation-ship to life" (p. 211), and on our feelings of confusion, loss, frus-tration, fear, anger, joy, and accomplishment.

For many of us, reflection includes revealing personal knowl-edge, feelings, beliefs, and values of which we may not have been previously aware. Reflection also includes becoming aware of our outside world—our families, friends, work, and community—in greater depth and breadth and relating our inside world (our knowl-edge, feelings, beliefs, and values) to it. Thus reflection can help us become whole people at the same time as we are becoming more able leaders.

The transition phase also includes unknowing. We wrestle with what we want to leave behind and what we want to move forward, and as we try to decide what of the new or the "other" we want to accept, we reach a stage of unknowing. For many people, unknow-ing is like a dark cave with dangers lurking in the shadows and the possibility of brilliant light and joy around the next turn. Unknowing simply means not knowing. And none of us, particularly if we have many years of academic preparation, do not want to not know. Transition often requires that we not know before we can know, that there be darkness before there can be light, that there be death before rebirth. Bridges (1991) says it this way: "People make the new beginning only if they have first made an ending and spent some time in the neutral zone. Yet most organizations try to start with the beginning rather than finishing with it. They pay no attention to endings. They do not acknowledge the existence of the neutral zone, then wonder why people have so much difficulty with change" (p. 6).

As we work through the transition phase, we may be thrown back to searching for new alternatives and may develop a new awareness that requires further analysis and pondering. Clearly, the transformation process is not linear; it allows for the constant moving back and forth among the various phases.

Leaders who have worked through the transition phase often talk about it as a peak experience or even a kind of rediscovery in their lives. Some refer to it as a spiritual experience. The decision–transition phase is clearly a major turning point for people who experience it. Several participants in the National Extension Leadership Development (NELD) program reported that they experienced transition as part of their development. One person described it this way: "There are times when [my experience with leadership development] brings on emotional highs different from anything I have experienced before. The trauma is that I finally decided that I have to confront my aspirations in my life. I have always avoided that issue. I have operated with the belief that I could take advantage of any situation in which I find myself. Now I am focusing on what differences I can make in the world and how I can do it. This is a dramatic shift in the way I think."

With transition comes a reaffirmation of old beliefs, values, and ideas; an acceptance and integration of new ones; and a discarding of obsolete ones.

Action

Now you are ready to try out your new ideas about leadership. As you try something different, from time to time you stop and reflect: Is what I am doing consistent with what I believe and feel about the requirements of leadership in my work context? What further changes do I need to make? What frustrations in my work continue?

With action and reflection, you may be tossed back to the decision–transition phase for further work, or you may develop a new, more sophisticated awareness and begin working through the entire transformation process again, this time at a deeper level.

For many leaders, moving from traditional approaches to newer approaches requires much more than simply identifying and attempting to mimic a different set of leadership skills. The ideas of leadership for the emerging age are built on a set of beliefs and values that allow leaders to face an uncertain future without recipes and how-to lists.

The NELD participant quoted earlier began with a problem— things were not going right for her—and confronting the problem led to awareness and then to other phases of the transformation process. Transformation can also occur when there is not a problem, at least not an immediate one. Everything in a leader's life may be humming along without a hitch. But a leader who is constantly exploring new leadership approaches may, in the midst of trying out a new approach, achieve a new awareness about her organization, her co-workers, and ultimately herself. Thus transformation may occur without premeditation.

Participants in the NELD program talked about transformation in a variety of ways. Transformation ordinarily occurred when leaders considered new ways of leading, discovered new ways of relating to people, and explored approaches to communication different from what they had used in the past. One of the participants reported, "Needless to say, I have been struggling with just about everything. I've always said that you only learn through adversity, and I'm putting that to the test." This person is in the midst of a major transformation as she looks at who she is, how she leads, and how the organization is reacting to her efforts. She has many new perspectives on leading and leadership. "More than anything, I have come to understand how fluid the process of leadership is. The notion that one can predict the outcome of a plan seems ridiculous to me. Leadership requires time, attention to details, understanding of both people and complex situations, the willingness to change one's mind, and taking risks, among other things. If one is not willing to work at it, one should not strive to be an administrative leader."

Other Transformations

In these stormy-weather times, not only do many leaders experience a transformation, but many organizations, colleagues, and participants do as well. Thus transformation is not a process relegated to individual leaders who are attempting to lead in new ways. Organizations experience the same stages of transformation outlined above as they attempt to move into the emerging age. I have described elsewhere the transformation process that higher education organizations are experiencing (Apps, 1988); the same process, with appropriate contextual modifications, of course, would apply to many adult education organizations.

Not only do leaders and organizations experience transformation, but the participants in adult education programs do too. This is particularly true for adult education organizations that have a relatively long history and a participant group that has dwindled in size but continues to support the organization and expects the familiar educational programs. As these organizations attempt to change, many longtime participants are shocked, angered, and thrown into transformation. An excellent example of this is the cooperative extension system, which has made substantial changes in how it programs and to whom it gives priority attention. In many states, traditional client groups—farmers, ranchers, and homemakers, for example—are upset with cooperative extension because it has moved into community development and nutrition education for low-income people in metropolitan areas.

As leaders experience transformation, their attempts to do things differently often frustrate colleagues accustomed to working with them as they were. When leaders attempt to lead differently, others are often pushed into transformation.

I could discuss several other examples of transformation that occur as leaders and organizations attempt to meet the challenges of the emerging age. Board members, taxpayers, advisory committees, donors of money to our programs, and others who have contact with us all have the potential for transformation as we and our organizations change.

Thus transformation is not merely something that leaders experience as they do their work differently. Multiple transformations occur, inside and outside the organization. A challenge for leaders is to realize that not only must they recognize and wrestle with their own transformation, but they must also be sympathetic and patient with others around them who are experiencing transformation.

Leaders can help others experiencing transformation in several ways. Keeping them informed about what is happening in a changing organization is one important approach. Rumors fly as an organization experiences change. Keeping people informed about what is happening helps squelch the rumors. In cases where there are clear endings—a program area is closed down, for example—mark the closing with a celebration. My nephew, a sailor, experienced the decommissioning of his ship. The Navy sponsored a celebration, gave each sailor a memento of the ship, and recounted its history through several naval engagements. Respecting what people have done in the past is one way to help them with their transformation.

The movement to a new perspective on adult education in most instances is more than an incremental change in what we have been doing. It involves a profound change in leaders, organizations, and the many people with whom the adult education organization has contact. People change significantly, as do the organizations that employ them. To move from the old perspective to the new one requires a transformation.

Chapter Twelve

Leadership for Change in Adult Education

The approach to leadership discussed in this book challenges adult education organizations, administrators, programmers, and participants in adult education programs. The challenges are both fundamental and applied.

Fundamental Challenges

First and foremost is the challenge to administrators, teachers, support people, advisory committees, and participants in adult education programs to wrestle with fundamentally new ways of thinking in the emerging age (see Chapter Two). Examples of new ways of thinking include attending to both-and rather than either-or—a merging of apparently opposing perspectives to gain the best of both and often to create a perspective that is more than either perspective on its own. New thinking includes accepting linear *and* nonlinear processes; accepting the need to grow *and* sustain; and considering approaches *and* goals, competition *and* cooperation, efficiency *and* effectiveness, specialization *and* generalization, parts *and* wholes, scientific knowledge *and* knowledge from other sources, consistency *and* paradox, scientific values and beliefs *and* personal values and beliefs, and predictable *and* nonpredictable change.

Other fundamental challenges include these:

- *Accepting paradox and ambiguity as reality rather than anomaly.* Too often we discount the paradoxical and the ambiguous because they don't fit our models and theories of thought. Yet it is here, in seemingly paradoxical and ambiguous situations, that new thought and direction often emerge. And it is in paradox and ambiguity that much of the reality of adult education and adult education leadership lies.

• *Developing more sophisticated perspectives about diversity*. Today diversity is too often seen as mandate, meeting the letter of the law or the stipulation of policy. We strive to employ members of minority groups in our programs. We advertise that our programs are open to everyone regardless of race, religion, occupation, and so on. But in our attempts to accommodate diversity, we often fail to recognize the power that comes from people of diverse perspectives. Organizations fail to realize that by integrating the diversity of culture, gender, race, and ethnicity in our programs, we have broadened our base of effectiveness manyfold, beyond the obvious goals of attracting people who might otherwise be uncomfortable participating.

• *Developing a global awareness*. Many adult education organizations have accepted the challenge of becoming citizens of the world. Others have remained parochial, attending to local needs and featuring local perspectives but failing to recognize the need to cross borders.

Thinking globally is a challenge that all adult education organizations face. In Chapter Four I explained how adult education leaders work in multiple contexts, including a global context. As one middle manager in a leadership development program asked, "Is nationalism just another 'ism,' like sexism or racism?" (Juan Moreno, personal correspondence, October 7, 1993).

How do we become citizens of the globe? This is a challenge that most of us have not thought much about. How can we put into practice a new perspective on global citizenship, where global border crossing is as easy as moving from one city to the next in our own country? Perhaps what is needed first is some border crossing in our minds that allows us to cross the border from thinking locally to thinking locally and globally at the same time.

• *Reconsidering empowerment. Empowerment* is a term used widely these days. Generally it means sharing power with those with whom we work or providing appropriate conditions so that people can harness the power they have for contributing to an organizational end. In both of these situations, empowerment is one-way, from an administrative leader to a staff person, for example.

But empowerment also means recognizing and accepting the power that people already have, without the intervention of an administrative leader. This recognition of the power inherent in people is fundamental to looking at diversity as a necessity rather than as an accommodation dictated by laws or policies. For instance, empowering minority group members who are on a staff or who attend classes and workshops means listening to their truth from their perspectives. Their power is not something that an administrator gives them. The administrative leader gains by accepting the power these people already have, as expressed in their truth.

When we who are of European roots attempt to provide programs for Native Americans, for example, we often err by not listening to their unique voices, which speak a truth that may be foreign to us or may contradict the truth that we believe everyone should hold. We may have a way of programming that we believe should fit all groups and cultures. A Native American community may prefer to organize their educational activities their way, and our role may be to provide resources or to be a partner in the educational endeavor rather than to serve as a provider.

• *Examining the basic elements of education.* To be consistent with the leadership approach suggested in this book, traditional ideas about education, teaching and learning, the role of teacher, and views about learners must be challenged. Education for the past seventy-five years has been greatly influenced by the industrial age (see Chapter Nine). It makes no sense to develop new structures for adult education organizations and prepare a new kind of leader if the essence of what we do—education—is not itself transformed. The emerging age requires fundamental changes in most aspects of the educational process, building on the best of the past and creating new approaches based on the assumptions of the emerging age.

Challenges for Leaders

Adopting the leadership approach embraced in this book is not without risks and challenges. Most leaders who participate in a leadership development program experience transformation. As explained in Chapter Eleven, transformation entails change and personal upheaval. Leaders experiencing transformation move from the familiar and known to the unfamiliar and often mysterious. During the transition phase of transformation, leaders confront the loss of the old and commit themselves to learning new beliefs and ways of doing things. In the process they celebrate the old beliefs and leadership approaches that fit the requirements of the emerging age, and they unlearn beliefs and behaviors that are no longer appropriate. In the process these leaders experience an emotional roller coaster, with highs and lows, periods of extreme anxiety interspersed with moments of calm.

During these times of turbulent personal change, leaders must remind themselves that transformation takes time. Reading a book, enrolling in a graduate course, or attending a workshop is not sufficient. Considerable thinking and wrestling with feelings are required, along with the opportunity to practice new approaches to leadership and reflect on the outcomes. Taking time to be alone, away from the pressures of work, is essential for meaningful reflection to take place.

Becoming a leader for the emerging age must be viewed more as a journey than a definite endpoint. It is a continuous process. And the process is not linear. It is punctuated by rapid movement forward, plateaus, and regression. Often the process seems more like a spiral, as similar themes are returned to again and again, each time at a deeper level of understanding.

In the midst of it all, considerable unlearning occurs as leaders wrestle with the relevance and appropriateness of old ideas, beliefs, and leadership approaches. The challenge is to continuously reflect on fundamental beliefs and values and keep an integrated personal credo statement for one's personal and work life. It is easy to be trapped into asking "What does the organization want me to do?" rather than "What do I want to be?" Keeping in control of who one is as leader and maintaining a sense of personal integrity are essential challenges. Of course, leaders listen to the organization's demands, but they also listen to their own.

Leaders must constantly challenge themselves to be whole people who work and play, who love and are loved, who enjoy family and community, who have interests beyond the workplace, and who know the mingling of mind, body, and spirit.

A challenge for many leaders is to be patient with themselves and what they are learning. Some participants in leadership development programs want immediate results. As they attempt to become a different kind of leader, they become impatient and frustrated when they face the reality of personal change and development.

The most difficult challenge of all, for leaders who want to lead in new ways, is to get up the courage to try new ideas. Only through trying the new ways of thinking and doing can leaders come to know them. And only through trying new leadership approaches can programs and organizations change.

Challenges for Organizations

As we confront the realities of the emerging age, with its many challenges, paradoxes, and ambiguities, organizations too face many challenges. For instance, organizations that have placed high priority on the development of their leaders must realize that these leaders need considerable support and encouragement, particularly when experiencing transformation. Sometimes an organization expects its leaders to perform immediately at some new and different level. Leaders experiencing transformation need organizational support and encouragement, not impatience and intolerance.

In leadership development programs of which I have been a part, a most difficult aspect is helping the people with whom the leader in transformation has contact to be patient and understanding. Too often supervisors expect such leaders to perform their work as usual—perhaps even more of it and more efficiently. Invariably, leaders in transformation are rethinking how they wish to lead, the approaches to use, the way in which they relate to people, and so on; to their supervisors they may appear confused and even less efficient than they were before.

Thus a challenge of preparing leaders for the emerging age, particularly when the preparation involves fundamental changes in beliefs, examination of basic values, and searching for new leadership approaches, is to assist supervisors, colleagues, and others with whom the leader has contact to understand the elements of this new approach to leadership and the phases of the transformation process. This is no small task. And the task can't be assumed solely by the leaders themselves. The entire organization, particularly supervisors, must assume an important role in understanding and support. Because transformation requires learning, and learning generally takes time, leaders need direct support. They require time away from the job and monetary support to attend meetings, buy books, participate in workshops, and the like.

In the National Extension Leadership Development program, which I recently directed, I recall talking to a prospective intern's supervisor, an extension director. He was reluctant to allow this middle manager to apply, for fear that she would spend too many hours away from her work. He said that he would agree to the woman's participation as long as she used her vacation time to attend the four one-week workshops that we conducted over the course of a year. I told him that we couldn't accept a participant under such conditions and that we expected the organization to support her with time off (not vacation time). The director then wondered if she needed to attend all the workshops, if maybe some of them would be more helpful than others. He proceeded to question me about the content of each workshop. I explained that the nature of the program was such that participants were expected to attend all four workshops and that the workshops were interrelated. Finally, he said he would think about it. Eventually the woman did apply and was accepted in the program. The director retired soon after.

In another instance, at one of our workshops an intern asked if she could talk with me privately. She explained that since she was accepted into the leadership development program, her relationship with her supervisor had deteriorated dramatically.

"Before this program," she said, "we got along fine. Now we scarcely speak to each other. He avoids me rather than seeking me out."

"Why do you suppose that is?" I inquired.

"I think he believes I'm after his job," she replied.

Unfortunately, some supervisors feel threatened by people developing new perspectives and new ways of leading, particularly if these new approaches conflict with the supervisor's style.

As Martha Tack (1991) points out, "We clearly must begin to nurture those who see the world differently and project a dramatically different future . . . , those who tend to shake things up rather than follow established precedents" (p. 30). An adult education administrator enrolled in the above-mentioned leadership development program said, "Some of the frustration I feel is trying new ideas and instigating change and then being told how wrong I am by those with whom I work." Fortunately, this administrator received outstanding support from his dean.

In addition to supporting leaders enrolled in leadership development programs, organizations entering the emerging age face many other challenges. A few are outlined here.

There is nothing more frustrating and challenging for leaders who are learning to lead differently than an organization so stuck in the past that it will do almost anything rather than change. Colleges and universities—an important segment of the organizations providing adult education—are among the most conservative of all institutions in society and the most reluctant to change. Yet the faculty of these institutions are often viewed as the most liberal and most forward-thinking people in the community. Paradoxically, when discussion of curriculum change, organizational adjustment, or any number of other issues arises, forward thinking flies out the window and is replaced by a scramble to protect the status quo at all costs.

Let's look at some of the challenges that must be met at colleges and universities:

• *Moving past the antiquated assumption that all knowledge should be organized by discipline and managed by departments.* It has been said often in recent years that people and communities have questions and problems, whereas universities have departments and disciplines. Attempts at interdisciplinary work have too often resulted in abysmal failure. For example, a low-income community organization comes to an adult education organization for assistance. The community has high levels of adult illiteracy, inadequate nutrition, less than satisfactory health service, and high unemployment. The adult education organization may send in a literacy specialist who organizes literacy classes, an economist who organizes workshops on economic development, a nutritionist who offers workshops on proper diet, and so on.

Seldom do the various "experts" talk to each other, and when they do they usually have difficulty understanding each other's perspectives and each other's jargon. No one, it seems, takes time to talk *with* the people because they are so busy talking *to* them. Often the people's indigenous knowledge about solving these problems is considerable, although the experts have difficulty hearing and accepting these alternative people-centered ideas. So the experts return to their adult education organization with comments about how difficult it is to reach these people, and the people's level of trust of adult education organizations drops one more notch. For colleges and universities to continue their roles in adult education, many need to rethink such basic questions as what knowledge is, how it should be organized, and how knowledge from various sources (including indigenous knowledge) can be included with research-based knowledge in an equitable way.

Another challenge is for adult educators to abandon the expert role, which often results in a one-way flow of knowledge, for a sharing role, wherein teacher and learner participate together in the learning, each learning from the other and each supporting and challenging the other.

- *Restructuring promotion and salary increase policies to encourage cooperative work as well as individual achievement and in the process recognize new ways of defining research and scholarship.* Ernest Boyer (1990, pp. 16–25) argues for an alternative approach to traditional ways of defining scholarship. He suggests four approaches: (1) scholarship of discovery (original research that contributes to human knowledge); (2) scholarship of integration (searching for new insight by bringing together and interpreting existing original research, often across disciplines); (3) scholarship of application (applying knowledge to solving problems and in the process, often reexamining the knowledge); and (4) scholarship of teaching (viewing teaching, with all of its challenges of seeking understanding and relationship between teacher and learner, as a scholarly activity).

- *Examining the concept of tenure and deciding where it serves a college or university well and where it prevents change and innovation.* For many years no one questioned tenure; hence tenure has long been a sacred cow that today desperately needs to be challenged. Too many colleges and universities hide behind tenure as a way to avoid change. Too many faculty hide behind tenure to avoid change as well. The future college and university will likely have a mixture of tenured and contract faculty—as is true at many institutions today. But the balance will be different. The numbers of tenured faculty will be relatively few and the contract faculty will be many.

- *Challenging continuing education units to relate in new ways to their home institutions, as well as to external groups.* For example, this may mean developing new approaches for sharing educational technology with the campus rather than investing in parallel equipment and carrying out parallel program development. One continuing education administrator said:

> Leaders for the emerging age need to be able to collaborate and build trusting relationships internally within their own organization and externally with other client groups and service providers. Leadership roles are frequently shifting from supervisor to communication roles, from controlling to networking, placing high value on negotiating skills and the ability to maintain a broad base of contacts. Internally, adult education leaders will have to deal with most of the academic units in their institution in order to provide logistical support for programs in which the unit is responsible for all curricular, staffing, and budgetary decisions. Further, they will probably have to work with the offices that provide admissions, registration, financial aid, library, and other services for regular on-campus programs, rather than running their own mini-version of all these services (Mary Jim Josephs, personal correspondence, March 17, 1994).

- *Rethinking programs for new and often overlooked audiences.*

Adult and continuing educators have difficulty acknowledging the simple fact that they have not dealt with the learning needs of the public but rather with the learning demands and requests of those able to pay fully for the teaching services, usually white upper-middle-class individuals seeking career advancement. We adult educators talk about the great value of our marginality in educational structures, citing the independence it gives us to respond rapidly to "learner needs," rather than acknowledging that being out of the budget mainstream has forced us to limit our response to those with the ability to pay up front, with no taxpayers' subsidy (Mary Jim Josephs, personal correspondence, March 17, 1994).

All adult education organizations, including colleges and universities, face several other practical challenges. Many organizations, particularly well-established ones, are buried under rules, regulations, and policies. To obtain approval for a new idea may take weeks of haggling. By the time the idea is approved, it may already be irrelevant.

David Osborne and Ted Gaebler (1993) say that organizations should be driven by their missions, not controlled by their rules. "We embrace our rules and red tape to prevent bad things from happening. . . . But those same rules prevent good things from happening. They slow [organizations] to a snail's pace. They make it impossible to respond to rapidly changing environments. They build wasted time and effort into the very fabric of the organization" (p. 111).

In my own organization, I'm constantly challenged about holding workshops in mountain hideaways, on Indian reservations, and in economically depressed areas of Alabama. "Why aren't you meeting in classrooms, like educators are supposed to do?" one of the keepers of our rules once said to me.

In many adult education organizations, programmers are controlled by the rules, not by the missions of their organizations. What few people want to consider is that rules were created by people, and they can be changed by people or eliminated to meet changing conditions. In addition to being paralyzed by rules, many adult education organizations are paralyzed by outmoded structures. As I discussed earlier, adult education organizations can no longer rely solely on a pyramidal form of organization structure. Only in the most traditional situations will we continue to see a pyramidal organization full of boxes with lines connecting them. Some organizations will resemble shamrocks, others a web, and still others an inverted pyramid. Structures will result from the context in which an organization finds itself, not because the organization has always been structured in a certain way

Challenges for Leadership Development Programs

Leadership development, in its many forms, is challenged to move beyond traditional approaches in which one person decides what a curriculum should be, to an interactive approach whereby both teachers and learners collectively decide what is taught.

Also, in many leadership development programs, leaders are put through extensive assessments to discover their strengths and weaknesses as leaders. In many programs, the leader is teamed with a "mentor" in a top administrative post. For example, in higher education, I am aware of a leadership program where leaders, hoping to become directors of college of agriculture research programs, are teamed with the current research program head. But as Tack (1991) points out, these programs "are insufficient because they are too frequently built on an ill-formulated model of mentorship, which assumes that the mentor is an effective leader" (p. 30). In many cases, the current administrator is not the appropriate mentor, even if doing a relatively good job. Leaders for the emerging age, as I have argued throughout this book, will have capacities and skills considerably different from those of many of today's administrators. Thus mentors must be carefully selected, often from outside the leader's current organization.

Likewise, assessment instruments, with some exceptions, are based on successful *current* leadership approaches. No one really knows what leadership approaches will be effective tomorrow. To provide the leadership that the emerging age of adult education will require, leadership development programs must themselves become transformed. The leadership development model that threads through this book is based on the assumption that leaders involved in a development program take charge of their own learning. They are challenged to develop their own learning plans (with the assistance of others, to be sure) and to carry them out. Most such leaders become quite different people in the process. They become transformed.

Guidelines for Leadership Development

Other guidelines for leadership development are outlined here.

- *Provide a combination of externally planned and self-directed activities.* I begin with the paradoxical assumption that all learners, certainly leaders, should discover how to take charge of their own learning. But at the same time I believe that for all of us, there is much that we do not know, and we are unaware that we do not know it. Being challenged by another person, reading, completing a leadership assessment instrument, participating in a workshop, visiting a foreign country, or living with people from another culture can all help us become aware of what we do not know.

At the same time, there is a dramatic difference between telling people what they should learn, a model often followed in education, and providing situations where participants, by themselves, become aware of what they do not know. In the second approach, learners remain in charge of their own learning. In the first, they become dependent on others to tell them what to learn.

In many educational programs, leadership development programs included, we err toward one extreme or the other. Many leadership development programs have a neatly organized curriculum that is well developed and sequenced, with little opportunity for learner participation in curriculum building. Some educational programs, including leadership development efforts, err in the opposite direction, instructing people to decide what they want to learn and then assisting them in their learning by providing resources. Little or no guidance is provided about what to learn. A mixture of the two approaches is desired—providing curricular structure and inviting participants to indicate their curriculum interests.

In leadership development programs that are planned over a year or longer, I encourage participants to develop a learning plan as described in Chapter Ten. This helps leaders become comfortable taking charge of their own learning. The reaction to developing a learning plan has been most interesting. Several participants told me that since they had never done anything like this before, they were feeling frustrated, perplexed, and challenged yet at the same time freed, in charge, and comfortable. Several said that after following their learning plan for a few weeks, they began to change and expand it. The process of developing the learning plan becomes one more way to help participants become conscious of what they did not know.

• *Encourage experiential as well as traditional learning activities.* Both planned and self-directed activities can reasonably include both approaches. For example, a short lecture is followed by people drawing pictures. A group discussing leadership approaches evolves into creating the group's concepts out of Lego blocks. A group studying perspectives on diversity lives with families in a housing development in a major urban area. Leaders studying team building and trust, after discussing the concepts, participate in a "high ropes" challenge course. Participants, of course, generally benefit by reading extensively, writing regularly, attending formal lectures, interviewing people, and traveling.

• *Encourage time for reflection.* Reflection allows people to get in touch with who they are, what they know, and what they believe. It also allows participants to consider what is outside of them, often at levels of depth and breadth they have not regarded previously. Reflection then provides participants with the opportunity to have a mental discussion between their inner selves and their outer worlds. Reflection is accomplished through solitude. In solitude people can confront themselves and what they are thinking and feeling, what they are experiencing, and what meaning it has for them. To assist with reflection during the workshops we conduct, we provide questions or prompts to help start the reflective juices flowing. Here are some examples of prompts used halfway through a ten-day workshop (Rossing and Neuman, 1993):

> Over the first four days, my thoughts have ranged from . . . to . . .
>
> At times I have felt . . . and at other times I felt . . .
>
> What I expected from the first four days was . . .
>
> What I received was . . .
>
> What surprised me the most was . . .
>
> What is a bit troubling for me is . . .
>
> Some things I learned or realized are . . .
>
> A few questions I now have are . . .
>
> Three words or phrases I would use to describe what I have experienced so far are . . .

• *Develop a program over time.* Too often leadership development is viewed as something that ought to be accomplished in a three-day workshop or, even worse, in an hourlong talk in the middle of some other in-service activity. It takes time to learn a new way of leading and to wrap one's mind around the new thinking and associated feelings.

One model I use for noncredit workshops includes an intensive five-day workshop, with mail, phone, e-mail, and other contact after the workshop, and then a follow-up face-to-face workshop six months after the first one. At the follow-up workshop, participants discuss new ideas they have tried, new concepts they are exploring, and barriers they faced as they tried to move in new directions. This model allows for study, reflection, action, and interaction, as well as the stimulus that a face-to-face workshop often provides.

For a yearlong leadership development model, we used "adviser-mentors" in positions different from the ones the participants held. For instance, a university department chair was teamed with the vice president of a corporation, and an extension associate director was teamed with the dean of continuing education at another institution. The adviser's role was to encourage, challenge, react to learning plans, provide ideas for reading and thinking, and in some instances serve as a role model.

• *Consider curriculum themes in a leadership development program.* In the National Extension Leadership Development intern program, our curriculum included four themes: developing a philosophy of leadership, developing capacity for organizational change and renewal, creating new understandings and feelings about diversity, and appreciating that we are all global citizens. To carry out these four themes, we planned workshops around each, lasting from five days to nearly two weeks. For example, we held a weeklong workshop on developing a learning plan and on creating a philosophy of leadership (including many of the ideas in this book). A second workshop several months later focused on organization renewal. A third workshop focused on diversity; it provided an opportunity for what we called "live diversity"—overnight stays with rural African-American families in central Alabama and Native American families on a reservation in North Dakota—and offered extensive workshops on the concept of parallel cultures and the meaning of diversity in society today. The fourth workshop focused on international understanding and becoming a global citizen. Two classes of interns visited the Netherlands and Belgium, becoming acquainted with the culture but also examining various aspects of the European Community (now the European Union) and its forward-looking challenges and plans. Certain interns visited Mexico, paying particular attention to trade relations between the United States and that nation. On this trip participants also had ample exposure to the local cultures, particularly the various economic and ethnic groups represented in the country.

In between the workshops, held over a twelve-month period, interns worked on other aspects of their personal learning plans. Almost all of them had extensive reading plans that ranged from studying various management functions—new approaches to budgeting and personal management, for example—to reading fiction that helped develop a deeper sense of culture, such as Toni Morrison's novel *Beloved*. Some interns visited private sector firms with specific questions in mind. One intern was interested in how a large company became smaller with minimum upheaval. This intern spent considerable time with the firm's administrative leaders as they worked through a process of reorganization. (See Adrian, 1993, for an in-depth description of the NELD program and how it was carried out.)

• *Encourage and support practical projects as part of a leadership development curriculum.* Through practical projects, put into effect in home organizations in most instances, participants in leadership development can try new leadership ideas, often outside the range of activities they have previously worked on. For instance, the intern mentioned above who was studying practical ideas for corporate downsizing applied many of the principles he was learning in his own organization as it faced budget cuts. Other interns have worked on such projects as diversity education within their own organizations and teaching administrators a "whole person" approach to work, recognizing family and community life along with work life. One intern's new interest in organizational change led him to join a university committee charged with refining the outreach function of the university.

The important feature of these application projects is that they encouraged participants in the leadership development program to try out new ideas in their home settings. Through discussions during the workshops, conversations with their advisers, and meetings with other interns between sessions, interns had an opportunity to fine-tune their projects and learn from what they were doing.

Without strongly encouraging interns to carry out practical projects as part of the leadership development program, some were reluctant and even fearful of trying out the new ideas of leadership they were learning. Strongly encouraging a practical project gives some participants the nudge they need to move past their initial feelings of fear about trying out their new learning.

These are but a few challenges that a new approach to leadership in adult and continuing education will create. I suspect that one of the greatest challenges of all is to constantly examine and challenge the approach to leadership discussed in this book. My hope is that the framework for leadership discussed here—which focuses on developing a personal philosophy of leadership and includes examining fundamental beliefs and values, considering a variety of leader qualities and characteristics, exploring several leadership approaches, and understanding perspectives on education—is sufficiently open that new approaches to leadership, beyond those suggested here, can emerge as new situations for leadership develop. The paradox presented is this: an approach to leadership requires a framework, but that framework should be viewed as freeing rather than confining. That is how I view the approach to leadership described in these pages. A framework is presented, with examples of how that framework may guide leaders. If we accept the ideas of discontinuous and unpredictable change, we must be willing—indeed, eager—to hang on this framework concepts that may be different from those I have described. Our challenge is not just to accept the framework I have described and the examples of its application, but to reflect constantly on whether the situation a leader faces is served by the examples. The unknown, chaotic future will require that and much more.

References

Adrian, J. G. *NELD Story: The First Three Years of the National Extension Leadership Development Program*. Madison: University of Wisconsin Extension, 1993.

Anderson, W. T. *Reality Isn't What It Used to Be*. San Francisco: HarperCollins, 1990.

Apps, J. W. *The Adult Learner on Campus*. Chicago: Follett, 1981.

Apps, J.W. *Study Skills for Adults Returning to School*. (2nd ed.) New York: McGraw-Hill, 1982.

Apps, J. W. *Improving Practice in Continuing Education: Modern Approaches for Understanding the Field and Determining Priorities*. San Francisco: Jossey-Bass, 1985.

Apps, J. W. *Higher Education in a Learning Society: Meeting New Demands for Education and Training*. San Francisco: Jossey-Bass, 1988.

Apps, J. W. *Mastering the Teaching of Adults*. Malabar, Fla.: Krieger/LERN, 1991.

Argyris, C. *Reasoning, Learning, and Action: Individual and Organizational*. San Francisco: Jossey-Bass, 1982.

Aslanian, C. B., and Brickell, H. M. *Americans in Transition: Life Changes as Reasons for Adult Learning*. New York: College Entrance Examination Board, 1980.

Astin, H. S., and Leland, C. *Women of Influence, Women of Vision: A Cross-Generational Study of Leaders and Social Change*. San Francisco: Jossey-Bass, 1991.

Bach, R. *Illusions*. New York: Dell, 1977.

Bass, B. M. *Bass and Stogdill's Handbook of Leadership*. (3rd ed.) New York: Free Press, 1990.

Baud, D., and Associates. *Reflection: Turning Experience into Learning*. London: Kogan Page, 1985.

Beder, H. (ed.). *Marketing Continuing Education*. New Directions for Continuing Education, no. 31. San Francisco: Jossey-Bass, 1986.

Belenky, M. F., and others. *Women's Ways of Knowing*. New York: Basic Books, 1986.

Bem, D. J. *Beliefs, Attitudes and Human Affairs*. Pacific Grove, Calif.: Brooks/Cole, 1970.

Bennett, W. *The Book of Virtues*. New York: Simon & Schuster, 1993.

Bennis, W. *On Becoming a Leader*. Reading, Mass.: Addison-Wesley, 1989.

Block, P. *The Empowered Manager: Positive Political Skills at Work*. San Francisco: Jossey-Bass, 1987.

Bolman, L. G., and Deal, T. E. *Reframing Organizations: Artistry, Choice, and Leadership*. San Francisco: Jossey-Bass, 1991.

Boone, E. J. *Developing Programs in Adult Education*. Englewood Cliffs, N.J.: Prentice Hall, 1985.

Boyer, E. *Scholarship Reconsidered: Priorities of the Professorate*. Princeton, N.J.: Carnegie Foundation for the Advancement of Teaching, 1990.

Boyle, P. G. *Planning Better Programs*. New York: McGraw-Hill, 1981.

Brandt, R. "On Rethinking Leadership: A Conversation with Tom Sergiovanni." *Educational Leadership*, Feb. 1992, pp. 46–49.

Bridges, W. *Managing Transitions*. Reading, Mass.: Addison-Wesley, 1991.

Burns, J. M. *Leadership*. New York: HarperCollins, 1978.

Capra, F. *The Turning Point*. New York: Bantam Books, 1983.

Capra, F. *The Tao of Physics*. New York: Bantam Books, 1991. (Originally published 1975.)

Cartwright, D., and Zander, A. *Group Dynamics Research and Theory*. New York: HarperCollins, 1953.

Cole, J. "From the Heart." *Sky*, Apr. 1992, pp. 18–22.

Conot, R. *A Streak of Luck: The Life and Legend of Thomas Alva Edison*. New York: Seaview Books/Simon & Schuster, 1979.

Courtenay, C. "An Analysis of Adult Education Administration Literature, 1936–1989." *Adult Education Quarterly*, 1990, 40(2), 63–77.

Covey, S. R. *The Seven Habits of Highly Effective People*. New York: Simon & Schuster, 1989.

Covey, S. R. *Principle-Centered Leadership*. New York: Summit Books, 1991.

Crandall, R. "Personal Passion: Door to Success." *New Leaders*, Sept.-Oct. 1993, p. 4.

Crauthers, J. "Continuing Education in the Learning Society: An Interview with Dr. Jerold Apps." *Canadian Journal of University Continuing Education*, 1991, 17(2), 55–68.

Cross, K. P. *Adults as Learners: Increasing Participation and Facilitating Learning*. San Francisco: Jossey-Bass, 1981.

Dawson, J. "Indian Science, Western Science: Different Views That Are Not Contradictory." *Minneapolis Star Tribune*, Oct. 18, 1992, pp. 1B, 5B.

De Mott, B. "Choice Academic Pork: Inside the Leadership-Studies Racket." *Harper's*, Dec. 1993, pp. 61–77.

De Pree, M. *Leadership Is an Art*. New York: Dell, 1989.

De Pree, M. *Leadership Jazz*. New York: Doubleday, 1992.

Desjardins, C., and Brown, C. O. "A New Look at Leadership Style." *Phi Kappa Phi Journal*, Winter 1991, pp. 18–20.

Dickens, C. *A Tale of Two Cities*. New York: Modern Library, 1950. (Originally published 1859.)

Drucker, P. *Managing for the Future*. New York: Dutton, 1992.

Edelson, P. J. (ed.). *Rethinking Leadership in Adult and Continuing Education*. New Directions for Adult and Continuing Education, no. 56. San Francisco: Jossey-Bass, 1992.

Eisner, E. W. *The Educational Imagination: On the Design and Evaluation of School Programs*. (2nd ed.) New York: Macmillan, 1985.

Estes, C. P. *Women Who Run with the Wolves*. New York: Ballantine, 1992.

Ferguson, M. *The Aquarian Conspiracy*. Los Angeles: Tarcher, 1980.

Freedman, L. *Quality in Continuing Education: Principles, Practices, and Standards for Colleges and Universities*. San Francisco: Jossey-Bass, 1987.

Gardner, J. W. *On Leadership*. New York: Free Press, 1990.

Gilligan, C. *In a Different Voice*. Cambridge, Mass.: Harvard University Press, 1982.

Giroux, H. A. *Border Crossings*. New York: Routledge, 1992.

Gleick, J. *Chaos: Making a New Science*. New York: Viking, 1987.

Greene, M. *Landscapes of Learning*. New York: Teachers College Press, 1978.

Greenleaf, R. K. *Servant Leadership: A Journey into the Nature of Legitimate Power and Greatness*. Mahwah, N.J.: Paulist Press, 1977.

Hagberg, J. O. *Real Power: Stages of Personal Power in Organizations*. San Francisco: HarperCollins, 1984.

Haiman, F. S. *Group Leadership and Democratic Action*. Boston: Houghton Mifflin, 1951.

Handy, C. *The Age of Unreason*. Boston: Harvard Business School Press, 1989.

Harman, W. *Global Mind Change*. Indianapolis: Knowledge Systems, Inc., 1988.

Heider, J. *The Tao of Leadership*. New York: Bantam Books, 1985.

Helgeson, S. *The Female Advantage: Women's Ways of Leadership*. New York: Doubleday, 1990.

Hoff, B. *The Tao of Pooh*. New York: Viking Penguin, 1982.

Hoff, B. *The Te of Piglet*. New York: Dutton, 1992.

Houle, C. O. *The Design of Education*. San Francisco: Jossey-Bass, 1972.

Hudson, F. M. *The Adult Years: Mastering the Art of Self-Renewal*. San Francisco: Jossey-Bass, 1991.

Hutchins, R. H. *The Learning Society*. New York: New American Library, 1968.

Kanter, R. M. *The Change Masters*. New York: Simon & Schuster, 1983.

Kerpan, M. L. "The 21st Century Challenge: Achieving Balance." *New Leaders*, Sept.-Oct. 1993, p. 3.

Knowles, M. *The Modern Practice of Adult Education*. (2nd ed., rev.) New York: Associated Press/Follett, 1980.

Knox, A. B. *Adult Development and Learning: A Handbook on Individual Growth and Competence in the Adult Years*. San Francisco: Jossey-Bass, 1977.

Knox, A. B. *Helping Adults Learn: A Guide to Planning, Implementing, and Conducting Programs.* San Francisco: Jossey-Bass, 1986.

Knox, A. B. "Leadership Challenges to Continuing Higher Education." In A *Handbook for Professional Development in Continuing Education.* Washington, D.C.: National University Continuing Education Association, 1990.

Knox, A. B. "Educational Leadership and Program Administration." In John M. Peters, Peter Jarvis, and Associates. *Adult Education: Evolution and Achievements in a Developing Field of Study.* San Francisco: Jossey-Bass, 1991.

Knox, A. B. (ed.). *Leadership Strategies for Meeting New Challenges.* New Directions for Continuing Education, no. 13. San Francisco: Jossey-Bass, 1982.

Knox, A. B., and Associates (eds.). *Developing, Administering, and Evaluating Adult Education.* San Francisco: Jossey-Bass, 1980.

Koestenbaum, P. *Leadership: The Inner Side of Greatness.* San Francisco: Jossey-Bass, 1991.

Kotter, J. P. *A Force for Change.* New York: Free Press, 1990.

Kouzes, J. M., and Posner, B. Z. *The Leadership Challenge: How to Get Extraordinary Things Done in Organizations.* San Francisco: Jossey-Bass, 1987.

Kouzes, J.M., and Posner, B.Z., *Credibility: How Leaders Gain and Lose It, Why People Demand It.* San Francisco: Jossey-Bass, 1994.

Kübler-Ross, E. *On Death and Dying.* New York: Macmillan, 1969.

Kuhn, T. S. *The Structure of Scientific Revolutions.* Chicago: University of Chicago Press, 1970.

Lewin, K., and Lippitt, R. "An Experimental Approach to the Study of Autocracy and Democracy: A Preliminary Note" *Sociometry,* 1937–1938, *1,* 292–300.

Lindeman, E. C. *The Meaning of Adult Education.* Montreal: Harvest House, 1961. (Originally published 1926.)

Luft, J. *On Human Interaction.* Palo Alto, Calif.: National Press Books, 1969.

Matkin, G. W. *Effective Budgeting in Continuing Education.* San Francisco: Jossey-Bass, 1985.

Merriam, S. B., and Caffarella, R. S. *Learning in Adulthood: A Comprehensive Guide.* San Francisco: Jossey-Bass, 1991.

Mintzberg, H. *The Nature of Managerial Work.* New York: HarperCollins, 1973.

Mitroff, I. M. *Break-Away Thinking.* New York: Wiley, 1988.

Morgan, G. *Images of Organizations.* Newbury Park, Calif.: Sage, 1986.

Moyers, B. *Healing and the Mind.* New York: Doubleday, 1993.

Nanus, B. *The Leader's Edge.* Chicago: Contemporary Books, 1989.

Nanus, B. "Futures: Creative Leadership." *Futurist,* May-June 1990, pp. 13–17.

Nanus, B. *Visionary Leadership: Creating a Compelling Sense of Direction for Your Organization.* San Francisco: Jossey-Bass, 1992.

Ortega y Gasset, J. *What Is Philosophy?* New York: Norton, 1960.

Osborne, D., and Gaebler, T. *Reinventing Government.* Reading, Mass.: Addison-Wesley, 1993.

Owen, H. *Riding the Tiger: Doing Business in a Transforming World.* Potomac, Md.: Abbott Publishing, 1991.

Palmer, P. *To Know as We Are Known: A Spirituality of Education.* New York: HarperCollins, 1983.

Palmer, P. *The Active Life: A Spirituality of Work, Creativity, and Caring.* New York: HarperCollins, 1990.

Palmer, P. "Remembering the Heart of Higher Education." Address at the American Association for Higher Education's National Conference on Higher Education, Washington, D.C., March 1993a.

Palmer, P. *To Know as We Are Known: Education as a Spiritual Journey.* (2nd ed.) San Francisco: HarperCollins, 1993b.

Patton, M. Q. *Qualitative Evaluation and Research Methods.* (2nd ed.) Newbury Park, Calif.: Sage, 1990.

Peck, M. S. *The Different Drum: Community Making and Peace.* New York: Simon & Schuster, 1987.

Peters, T. *Thriving on Chaos.* New York: Knopf, 1987.

Pigors, P. *Leadership or Domination.* Boston: Houghton Mifflin, 1935.

Quinn, R. E. *Beyond Rational Management: Mastering the Paradoxes and Competing Demands of High Performance.* San Francisco: Jossey-Bass, 1988.

Rosener, J. B. "Ways Women Lead." *Harvard Business Review,* Nov.-Dec. 1990, pp. 119–125.

Ross, M. G., and Hendry, C. E. *New Understandings of Leadership.* New York: Associated Press, 1957.

Rossing, B., and Neuman, T. "Evaluation Instrument." In *National Extension Leadership Development Program.* Madison: University of Wisconsin Extension, 1993.

Schein, E. H. *Organizational Culture and Leadership.* (2nd ed.) San Francisco: Jossey-Bass, 1992.

Schön, D. A. *The Reflective Practitioner.* New York: Basic Books, 1983.

Senge, P. M. *The Fifth Discipline.* New York: Doubleday, 1990.

Simerly, R. G., and Associates. *Strategic Planning and Leadership in Continuing Education: Enhancing Organizational Vitality, Responsiveness, and Identity.* San Francisco: Jossey-Bass, 1987.

Smith, D. H., and Offerman, M. J. "The Management of Adult and Continuing Education." In S. B. Merriam and P. M. Cunningham (eds.), *Handbook of Adult and Continuing Education.* San Francisco: Jossey-Bass, 1989.

Solomon, J. "A Touching Presidency." *Newsweek*, Feb. 22, 1993, p. 44.

Sperry, R. "Changing Priorities." *Annual Review of Neuroscience*, 1981, 4, 1–15.

Srivastva, S., Cooperrider, D. L., and Associates. *Appreciative Management and Leadership: The Power of Positive Thought and Action in Organizations.* San Francisco: Jossey-Bass, 1990.

Storr, A. *Solitude: A Return to Self.* New York: Free Press, 1988.

Strother, G. B., and Klus, J. P. *Administration of Continuing Education.* Belmont, Calif.: Wadsworth, 1982.

Tack, M. W. "Future Leaders in Higher Education." *National Forum*, 1991, 71(1), 29–32.

Tead, O. *The Art of Leadership.* New York: McGraw-Hill, 1935.

Tichy, N. M., and Devanna, M. A. *The Transformational Leader.* New York: Wiley, 1986.

United States Bureau of the Census. *Current Population Reports*, series P-25, no. 1018. Washington, D.C.: Government Printing Office, 1989.

Vaill, P. B. *Managing as a Performing Art: New Ideas for a World of Chaotic Change.* San Francisco: Jossey-Bass, 1989.

Wheatley, M. J. *Leadership and the New Science.* San Francisco: Berrett-Kohler, 1992.

Wlodkowski, R. J. *Enhancing Adult Motivation to Learn: A Guide to Improving Instruction and Increasing Learner Achievement.* San Francisco: Jossey-Bass, 1993.

Zinsser, W. *Writing to Learn.* New York: HarperCollins, 1988.

Index